Britain's Royal Family
in the Twentieth Century

Above Queen Elizabeth II with the Lord
Mayor of London on her Silver Jubilee
walkabout in June 1977.

Endpapers The Royal Family at Balmoral in 1972.

Overleaf The wedding of Edward Prince of
Wales and Princess Alexandra which took
place in 1863 at St George's Chapel, Windsor.
Queen Victoria, still in mourning for Albert,
watched the service from the gallery high
above the altar.

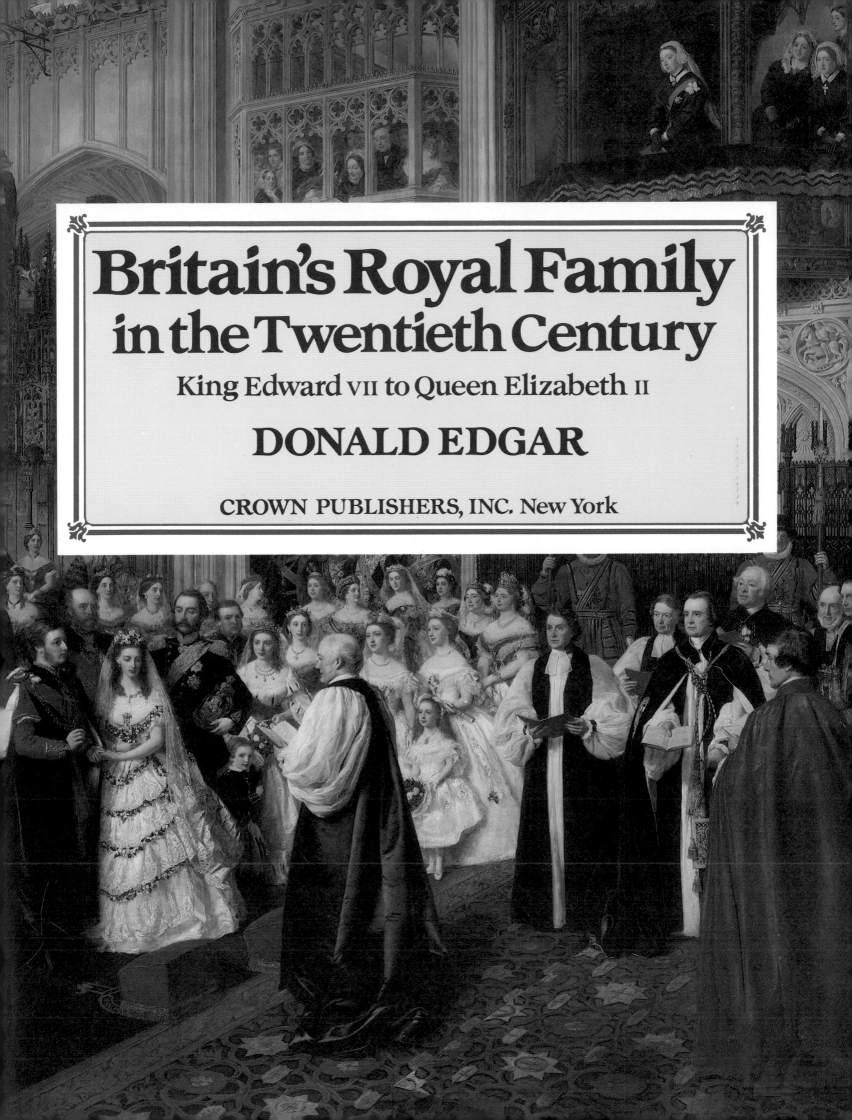

Britain's Royal Family in the Twentieth Century

King Edward VII to Queen Elizabeth II

DONALD EDGAR

CROWN PUBLISHERS, INC. New York

Contents

First English edition published by Artus Books Ltd, 1979
Copyright © MCMLXXIX by Artus Books Ltd
Library of Congress Catalog Card Number: 78–20652
All rights reserved.
First published by Crown Publishers, Inc. in the U.S.A. 1979
by arrangement with Weidenfeld (Publishers) Limited.
Printed and bound by L.E.G.O. Vicenza Italy

Library of Congress Cataloging in Publication Data

Edgar, Donald.
    Britain's royal family in the 20th century.

    Includes index.
    1. Great Britain—Kings and rulers—Biography.
2. Great Britain—History—20th century—Biography.
3. Monarchy, British. 4. Windsor, House of.
5. Great Britain—Royal household.   I. Title.
DA28.1.E32   1979   941.082'092'2 [B]   78–25923
ISBN 0–517–539411

Opposite George VI and Queen Elizabeth with the Princesses Elizabeth and Margaret at their home Royal Lodge, Windsor. A painting by James Gunn, 1950.

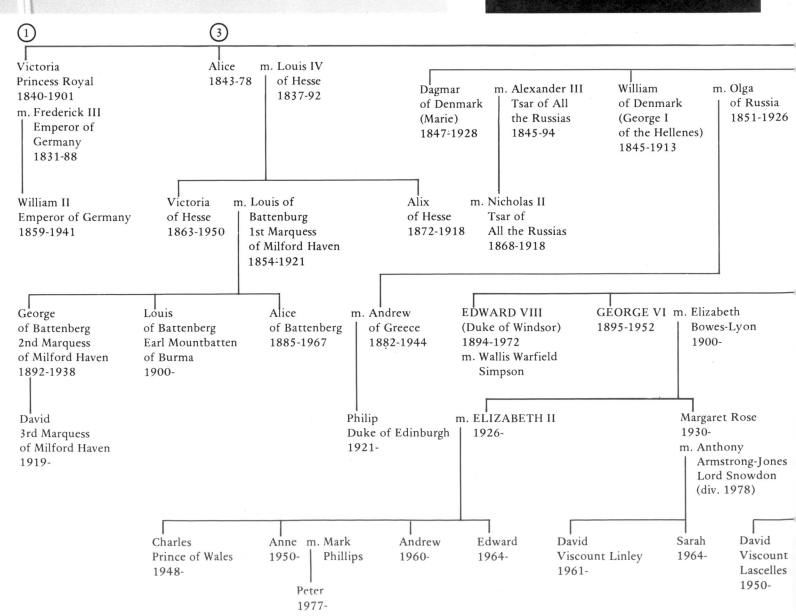

① ③

Victoria
Princess Royal
1840-1901
m. Frederick III
Emperor of
Germany
1831-88

Alice   m. Louis IV
1843-78   of Hesse
1837-92

Dagmar   m. Alexander III   William   m. Olga
of Denmark   Tsar of All   of Denmark   of Russia
(Marie)   the Russias   (George I   1851-1926
1847-1928   1845-94   of the Hellenes)
1845-1913

William II
Emperor of Germany
1859-1941

Victoria   m. Louis of
of Hesse   Battenburg
1863-1950   1st Marquess
of Milford Haven
1854-1921

Alix   m. Nicholas II
of Hesse   Tsar of
1872-1918   All the Russias
1868-1918

George   Louis   Alice   m. Andrew   EDWARD VIII   GEORGE VI   m. Elizabeth
of Battenberg   of Battenberg   of Battenberg   of Greece   (Duke of Windsor)   1895-1952   Bowes-Lyon
2nd Marquess   Earl Mountbatten   1885-1967   1882-1944   1894-1972   1900-
of Milford Haven   of Burma   m. Wallis Warfield
1892-1938   1900-   Simpson

David   Philip   m. ELIZABETH II   Margaret Rose
3rd Marquess   Duke of Edinburgh   1926-   1930-
of Milford Haven   1921-   m. Anthony
1919-   Armstrong-Jones
Lord Snowdon
(div. 1978)

Charles   Anne   m. Mark   Andrew   Edward   David   Sarah   David
Prince of Wales   1950-   Phillips   1960-   1964-   Viscount Linley   1964-   Viscount
1948-   1961-   Lascelles
1950-

Peter
1977-

The Houses of Saxe-Coburg-Gotha and Windsor

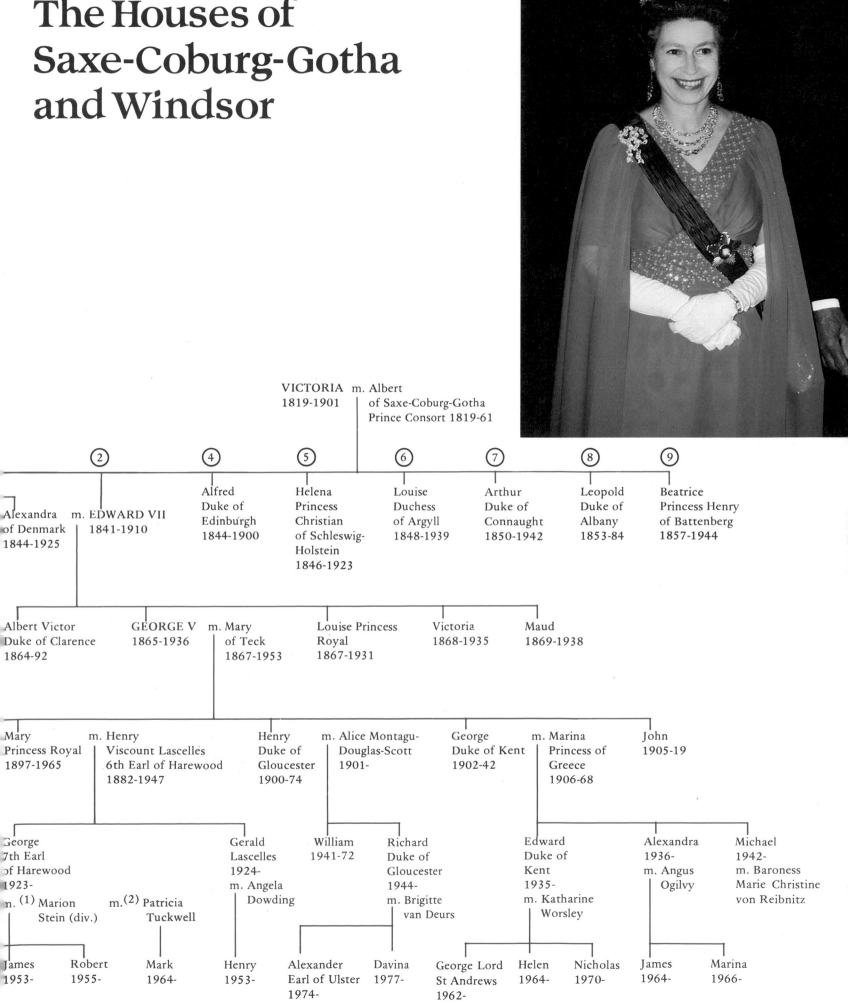

VICTORIA m. Albert
1819-1901   of Saxe-Coburg-Gotha
Prince Consort 1819-61

② ④ ⑤ ⑥ ⑦ ⑧ ⑨

Alexandra of Denmark 1844-1925 m. EDWARD VII 1841-1910	Alfred Duke of Edinburgh 1844-1900	Helena Princess Christian of Schleswig-Holstein 1846-1923	Louise Duchess of Argyll 1848-1939	Arthur Duke of Connaught 1850-1942	Leopold Duke of Albany 1853-84	Beatrice Princess Henry of Battenberg 1857-1944

Albert Victor Duke of Clarence 1864-92   GEORGE V 1865-1936 m. Mary of Teck 1867-1953   Louise Princess Royal 1867-1931   Victoria 1868-1935   Maud 1869-1938

Mary Princess Royal 1897-1965 m. Henry Viscount Lascelles 6th Earl of Harewood 1882-1947   Henry Duke of Gloucester 1900-74 m. Alice Montagu-Douglas-Scott 1901-   George Duke of Kent 1902-42 m. Marina Princess of Greece 1906-68   John 1905-19

George 7th Earl of Harewood 1923- m.(1) Marion Stein (div.) m.(2) Patricia Tuckwell   Gerald Lascelles 1924- m. Angela Dowding   William 1941-72   Richard Duke of Gloucester 1944- m. Brigitte van Deurs   Edward Duke of Kent 1935- m. Katharine Worsley   Alexandra 1936- m. Angus Ogilvy   Michael 1942- m. Baroness Marie Christine von Reibnitz

James 1953-   Robert 1955-   Mark 1964-   Henry 1953-   Alexander Earl of Ulster 1974-   Davina 1977-   George Lord St Andrews 1962-   Helen 1964-   Nicholas 1970-   James 1964-   Marina 1966-

Introduction

The British monarchy in the present century provokes two overriding reflections. The first is how singularly fortunate Britain has been in the royal incumbents of the throne. The second is how fortunate have been the sovereigns in a complaisant and tolerant British public, and in the guiding hands of their political advisers and successive governments. In a crisis all have kept their heads, which is more than can be said of most of the various monarchs with whom the twentieth century started. Indeed, the reign of George v saw the disappearance of five emperors, eight kings and eighteen more ruling dynasties.

It is a commonplace that the monarchy today has no real political power. A century ago, Walter Bagehot wrote of the sovereign's right to be consulted, right to encourage and right to warn. And in our democracy policy must, in the last analysis, rest with the prime minister and government of the day. It is Britain's good fortune that the transition to such a purely constitutional role has taken place so painlessly and so smoothly, and it says much for the commonsense of sovereigns and governments alike. To the twentieth century belongs much of the final process. Queen Victoria had, until her last years, taken an active interest in political matters and often attempted to influence political decisions. But Edward VII, who came to the throne almost at the start of the new century, in January 1901, acted differently. He was basically little interested in the routine trivia of domestic policies, and, where he had settled views on foreign affairs, these were generally in accord with British foreign policy anyway.

To George V, who came to the throne in 1910, is due much of the credit for moving the monarchy into its present role. He always acted scrupulously on the advice of his ministers and managed to keep the monarchy neutral, and hence above party politics, in all the burning political issues of the day. Since these issues involved momentous matters – such as the reform of the House of Lords, the constitutional position of Ireland, the rise of the Labour Party and the first Labour government, the General Strike and the first great step from Empire to Commonwealth – it can be seen how great has been the achievement. George VI and Elizabeth II have subsequently followed along this constitutional path with the result that Britain, the first country to unleash those forces of industrialism and socialism which have dethroned so many sovereigns, has today, paradoxically, a secure, stable and widely loved monarchy.

Opposite Queen Victoria with the five-year-old Prince Edward. A formal portrait painted by Winterhalter in 1846.

If constitutionally the monarch has become something of a royal cipher, public interest has focused intensely on the characters of the sovereigns themselves and of their families. More than anything else, British royalty in this century has symbolized the benefits and tranquility of a settled family life. Gracious without being arrogant, simple without being plebeian, Britain's royalty has had a stabilizing influence in a world charged with change, a world in which Britain has declined from great empire to minor power, and in which a new social structure has emerged to obliterate all but some external trappings of the society of 1900.

Not that royalty is without its critics, nor that criticism may not be justified, although it is an irony that theoretically the most powerful person in the land is the most powerless to counter such attacks. It was said of Edward VII that he spent his money on fast women and slow horses, and while the former may have gone out of fashion, the male members of Britain's Royal Family subsequently seem often to have derived considerable pleasure and satisfaction not only from equestrian pursuits but also from shooting countless birds and animals. The Gilbertian character for whom 'art stopped short at the cultivated court of the Empress Josephine' would find little to disabuse him in our twentieth-century royal Courts, while George V's love of stamp-collecting was as far as a sovereign this century appears to have gone towards a genuine intellectual pursuit.

But for all such criticisms, the monarchy has served the country well. Nowhere was this seen better than during the two World Wars, when first George V and then his son became the symbols for the fight for 'king and country'. There can be no doubt, of course, that victory in both wars strengthened the monarchy, just as defeat signalled the collapse of so many royal Houses elsewhere.

The world on which the twentieth century dawned was a world dominated by Europe, by great European-based empires and by kings and emperors. Today, as we approach the last two decades of the century, there is little except the historical record to remind us of this vanished age. The Austro–Hungarian, the Turkish and the Russian empires collapsed as a result of the First World War; and almost nothing now remains of the vast, extra-European territories then controlled by Britain, France, Germany, Holland, Belgium, Portugal and Spain. The First World War saw a wholesale shedding of crowned heads, most significantly the Hohenzollerns in Germany, Habsburgs in Austria–Hungary and Romanovs in Russia. Indeed, it became axiomatic that absolute rulers tended to disappear absolutely. Since then the process has continued, and today, outside Britain, only a handful of lesser states still owe allegiance to a sovereign. These surviving sovereigns, moreover, have only nominal powers. Everywhere they are sovereign in name only, little more than constitutional figureheads whose functions are almost entirely ceremonial. The centre of political gravity has also shifted markedly from Europe. The United States of America and the Soviet Union, perhaps soon to be joined by China and Brazil, are the super powers of today.

Queen Victoria and Prince Albert with three of their five children. A detail from Winterhalter's portrait, 1846. Albert had an unofficial but exceptionally powerful influence on Parliament during Victoria's reign.

The British monarchy has survived the royal holocausts, but it has inevitably undergone profound changes, due far more to factors external to the monarchy than to the characters of the monarchs themselves. And so the individual sovereigns in the twentieth century have to be viewed against this changing background.

Europe's crowned heads and aristocratic families gave to the world of 1900 a spurious appearance of stability. Beneath the surface, many forces were at work that were shortly to shatter the system. Industrialization and urbanization were bringing new political and social alignments. The middle classes challenged the aristocracy, and the working classes, inspired in some countries by the writings of Karl Marx, challenged both. Democratic and Socialist movements sounded the death knell for absolute monarchy. If monarchy could not adapt, it had to go.

Long before 1900, of course, enormous cracks had appeared in Europe's monarchical edifice. France had had no king since 1848 and had been a republic since 1871. But despite the republican movements which from time to time asserted themselves, the sovereigns and the ruling caste they supported usually managed to hold on. Tsar Nicholas II in St Petersburg and Emperor Franz Josef II in Vienna still maintained near absolute power. In Berlin the Kaiser, Wilhelm II, could still appoint and dismiss his own ministers.

In Britain, however, things were very different. Throughout the nineteenth century, and for long before that, the power of British monarchs had been steadily eroded. The erosion was largely one of custom and precedent, for although Britain might be said to have a constitutional monarchy, no written constitution has ever delineated the respective powers of sovereign, parliament, cabinet and people.

When Queen Victoria ascended the throne in 1837, not only was the monarch's influence potentially considerable but there were areas where such influence could, in practice, be felt. Indeed, her husband, Prince Albert, was said by Lord John Russell to be an informal but potent member of all Cabinets. The Queen herself paid meticulous attention to affairs of state. Yet the room for monarchical manœuvre was perceptibly whittled away. In 1900 Queen Victoria still reigned, but constitutional practice had by now firmly limited the areas within which the sovereign could act, and these were narrow in the extreme. It is at once an irony and an explanation that Europe's weakest monarchy should survive the turmoil of the twentieth century and should enter the last quarter of the twentieth century with as secure a foundation as at any time for two hundred years. For the British monarchy has continued to adapt to change and thus has managed to survive.

When Edward VII ascended the throne in 1901, the monarchy was already a very different institution from that which had existed at Queen Victoria's accession. Even Edward was more powerful than his successors. When Queen Elizabeth II came to the throne in 1952, the first twentieth-century British monarch to be born after Queen Victoria's reign, the transformation of the monarchy into a purely titular and ceremonial institution was complete.

Queen Victoria sketching at Loch Laggan with Prince Edward. A detail from a painting by Landseer, 1847.

The wedding
procession of
Edward and
Alexandra in 1863.
The procession is
passing through
Temple Bar on its
way to Windsor.

The history of the twentieth-century monarchy in Britain thus evolves against a background of declining political authority. Yet it evolves also against a background of considerable and perhaps growing public affection and esteem. The more withdrawn the sovereign has been from politics, the more the role of the sovereign as a figurehead above politics has been enhanced. The basis for popular approval of the monarchy lies not only with the twentieth-century sovereigns themselves but also with Queen Victoria. In the middle years of the 1860s the British monarchy was distinctly unpopular. Queen Victoria's husband, the German Prince Albert, had not commended himself to the majority of the British public, with his very un-British liking for culture and education and with the German influence that naturally prevailed at Court. After his sudden death in 1861, the Queen herself became a somewhat sullen recluse, and her remoteness from her subjects again brought the monarchy into disrepute. Gradually, however, age and circumstances made the Queen herself a beloved institution, and by the time of her great jubilees in 1887 and 1897 she aroused very real affection among the British people. At the time of her death, the mourning and grief demonstrated by all classes throughout the nation was deep and sincere. The people doubtless felt, as they watched the solemn funeral procession or read their black-edged newspapers, that they were witnessing not simply the passing of a loved queen but the passing also of an age.

The twentieth-century monarchy may therefore be seen in very broad terms as an institution which has exchanged the last vestiges of political influence for more and more ceremonial functions, royal patronage and good-will tours. In this ambassadorial role the monarchy has taken on a governmental function while remaining at the same time above politics. Withdrawn thus from the passions of politics, the monarchy attracts little overt republican hostility and remains a firmly entrenched part of national life.

The origins of the changes belong, of course, to a remote past. They move through the Magna Carta in 1215, through the Civil War in the seventeenth century when King Charles I unsuccessfully challenged the authority of parliament, through the Glorious Revolution of 1688 and through the course of the eighteenth century when, under the Hanoverian Georges, monarchical powers were eroded further in practice even though in theory they remained virtually limitless.

The twentieth century, too, has seen forces of its own which have served politically to weaken, if institutionally to strengthen, the monarchy. Three major elements may here be singled out. In the first place, the demise of kingship in so many countries has undoubtedly isolated the remaining royal families and pushed them further and further into a cocoon world. Before 1914, the large numbers of royalty meant frequent royal gatherings at weddings, funerals and christenings, and numerous state and informal visits. Ties of kinship linked most of the great ruling Houses. Queen Victoria was often called 'the grandmother of Europe', and when King Edward VII ascended the throne, one nephew, Wilhelm, was German Emperor, another, Nicholas II, was Tsar of Russia. A glance at old photographs shows many striking resemblances among Europe's ruling Houses. And since at the opening of the twentieth century many rulers were themselves exceedingly powerful – like the Tsar and the Kaiser – this fact in itself lent special significance to royal meetings, even with the British constitutional monarch. Family ties and the complexities of diplomatic protocol often made it easier for direct contact to be made between heads of state by royal meetings than through normal government channels. Foreign sovereigns and governments frequently failed to understand the true importance of the British monarchy. The King *seemed* powerful, and this assumption itself lent to the British monarchy a prestige which came from the authority of his relatives rather than from himself.

A second element which has reduced the political influence of the sovereign has been the rise of clearly defined political parties, for the monarch cannot show partiality between rival political factions. Edward VII was the first monarch to come to the throne with a fully-fledged party system in operation, and, as the present century has progressed, the divisions of issues on party lines have become ever more rigid. Reinforcing this has been the rise of the Labour Party and the consequent division of British politics on a broad class basis. Any bias shown now, as Queen Victoria showed successively for the Whig Lord Melbourne and the Tory Benjamin Disraeli, would clearly be interpreted as prejudice, not simply on personal or political grounds but on grounds of class.

The third element has been the decline in aristocratic rule shown, above all, by the diminishing power of the House of Lords. When the twentieth century opened, the House of Lords possessed in theory equal powers with the House of Commons. But these powers, after protracted and bitter struggles, have now been sharply diminished. The hereditary principle itself has therefore been undermined, and thus, though the monarchical arch may remain, the aristocratic supports have been removed. It is revealing that when Edward VIII, as Duke of Windsor, wrote his memoirs, he should say, 'Mine is the story of the life of a man brought up in a special way, as a Prince trained in the manners and maxims of the nineteenth century for a life that had all but disappeared by the end of his youth.'

The erosion of royal authority has, of course, brought gains as well as losses. The clear independence and neutrality of twentieth-century monarchs has kept them free from political fights and in consequence allows them to appear as true representatives of all the people of every class. Without doubt, too, the characters of the sovereigns themselves have played a major part in the affection and regard with which the monarchy is at present held. The world of the mass media which is the twentieth century, where every member of the Royal Family comes under public gaze and scrutiny on so many occasions, cannot be an easy one in which to live as a member of royalty. Yet, as we shall see, the twentieth-century sovereigns have, by and large, coped very well.

Opposite Portraits of Victoria at different stages of her life, and of her eldest children, the Prince of Wales with his sister Victoria, the Princess Royal, and their consorts and children, and her grandson George Duke of York with his consort and eldest child. A page from the special Diamond Jubilee edition of the *Illustrated London News* published in 1897.

CHAPTER ONE

Edward VII

Queen Victoria's long reign came to an end on 22 January 1901. 'Bertie', as Albert Edward, Prince of Wales, was known to his family, at last became king. He had waited a long time. He was already fifty-nine when he ascended the throne, and, in the event, his reign was not destined to be a long one. It lasted a mere nine years.

Despite its brevity, Edward VII's reign has acquired a character and an aura all of its own. The term 'Edwardian Age' conjures up a golden period, a time of gaiety and relaxation, in merciful contrast both to the sombre morality of the Victorian period and to the shattering events which so soon overtook the nation. Edward and his Court symbolized the age. Victoria's death ended a period of mourning for her beloved consort, Albert, which had lasted for well nigh forty years. Throughout this time Victoria had lived the life of a recluse, rarely visiting London, moving sedately with the seasons between Windsor, Balmoral and Osborne on the Isle of Wight. Buckingham Palace remained virtually a mausoleum to the dead Prince.

Edward, by contrast, loved pageantry and ceremonial. One of his first acts was to modernize Buckingham Palace and take up residence there, and so he was much closer and more in evidence to his subjects than his mother had been. His obvious fondness for pretty women also breathed some human life and earthly values into the rarified atmosphere of the royal Court.

Though advanced in years, Edward was astonishingly ill-prepared for the role he had to assume. His experience of life contrasted oddly with his inexperience of statecraft. The Queen had done little to initiate him into the intricacies of monarchy. Indeed, Victoria and Albert must share a great deal of blame for Edward's failings both as man and as sovereign.

The heir to the throne was born on 9 November 1841 at St James's Palace. He was twenty-five days old when he was created Prince of Wales. The young Prince's childhood years were to be wretched. His parents showed him little affection and understanding, and he was frequently compared unfavourably with his more intelligent and personable brothers and sisters. Albert and Victoria made little secret of their preference for Edward's older sister, Vicky, while all the royal children were constantly exhorted by their mother to live up to the standards set by the Prince Consort, paragon of all virtues. The

Opposite Edward VII in his full majesty as King and Emperor. A painting by Sir Luke Fildes, R.A.

Queen wrote to her uncle Leopold of Belgium shortly after Edward's birth: 'You will understand how fervent are my prayers, and I am sure everybody's must be, to see him resemble his father in *ever* *every* respect, both in body and mind.' And she later wrote to her s

None of you can *ever* be proud enough of being the *child* of such who has not his *equal* in this world – so great, so good, so faultle to follow in his footsteps and don't be discouraged, for to everything like him *none* of you, I am sure, will ever be. Try, th like him in *some* points, and you will have *acquired a great*

Edward was still a baby when plans were l
education. The Queen and the Prince Consc
exceedingly seriously. They consulted r
educationalists, Church dignitaries and poli
should be the appropriate education for
guiding hand in Edward's education w
a close friend of the royal family, the
Baron's views were very much in
her husband. Education was to
cultural background necess?
standards of moral rectitud
fear, or royal obsession, w
leanings of his great-un
was well in evidenc
existence of the m
wrote Albert in
govern, the we'
    Prince Alk
strenuous
mature
a staff
the
d

by his tutors and studied intently by the disappointed Albert. The regime under which Edward grew up meant that he had no contact with boys of his own age and, apart from his royal brothers and sisters, experienced only the company of adults.

Not surprisingly, Edward, who in any case had little inherent intellectual ability or natural affinity for the arts, reacted strongly. He became sullen, prone to occasional fits of ungovernable temper, and unco-operative with his tutors. The royal parents only took this as a sign that more discipline and application were necessary. They dismissed Birch, of whom Edward had grown fond, and appointed a new tutor, Frederick Gibbs, whose views on education were even stricter than those of his predecessor, and which coincided more exactly with those of Stockmar and Albert.

Edward was now ten, and his lessons were increased to six hours a day for six days a week, and light reading, such as the novels of Walter Scott, was banned.

There were, of course, occasional outings and treats, though always Edward was guarded closely lest he become infected with the moral looseness of the outside world. At thirteen he was allowed to accompany his parents to Paris. It was an indelible experience. He hero-worshipped the Emperor and adored the Empress Eugénie, and when the time came to depart pleaded that he and his sister be allowed to spend a few days further alone. The Empress replied that she was afraid his parents could not do without them, to which Edward responded: 'Don't fancy that, for there are six more of us at home and they don't want *us*.'

This early experience of a foreign land, with its welcome relief from the harsh regimentation of home, gave Edward a lifelong interest in travel. He went to Berlin in 1858 and toured Italy in 1859 and Canada and the United States in 1860. By this time his natural love of social life and his personal qualities of charm, good humour and tact were beginning to assert themselves. They further developed during his years at university when, at his father's insistance, he attended Oxford, Cambridge and Edinburgh. Edward was allowed little liberty. He lived apart from the other undergraduates and wore a special gown, and when he entered lectures the undergraduates were obliged to stand until the Prince of Wales had taken his seat.

Yet Edward responded not so much to the presence of academic luminaries as to the society of young men of fashion from which his closely confined existence could not wholly remove him. The Prince quickly acquired tastes for good food, wine, cigars, hunting, cards, expensive clothes and various other worldly pleasures which Albert and Stockmar had striven so hard to obliterate.

But worse was to come. In 1861 Edward managed to get permission to break his studies at Cambridge and to spend ten weeks with the Grenadier Guards at the Curragh Camp near Dublin. Albert insisted that his son should have the rank of a staff colonel and be subjected to a rigorous detailed programme, while the Prince had imagined himself as a simple subaltern, gradually getting to know the ropes from contemporaries. In November of that year, Edward having returned from Ireland to Madingley Hall in Cambridge, where he led his confined existence, Prince Albert heard a rumour that his son had had an affair at the Curragh with an actress, Nellie Clifden. The shocked Prince Consort decided that Edward must go on an extended overseas tour as soon as possible and brought forward plans for his son to visit the Near East. On 25 November Albert (already ill with typhoid) went to Cambridge to talk with Edward. Within three weeks, the Prince Consort was dead. A distraught Victoria wrote: 'That boy ... I never can, or shall, look at him without a shudder.'

For the rest of her long life the Queen remained devoted to the memory of her husband, and she spent much of the time in mourning and in seclusion. But in deference to Albert she kept the reins of statecraft firmly in her own hands. No political duties were allowed to devolve on Edward, and the Prince of Wales was denied access to official papers. On the other hand, Victoria's detestation of travel meant that Edward was increasingly called upon to represent the Queen at various functions at home and abroad, and it is possible to

Princess Alexandra riding on Viva, a portrait by Jean Edouard Lacretelle.

The three daughters of Edward and Alexandra, painted by S.P. Hall in 1893. They are, from left to right, Louise, who married the Duke of Fife and was very happy; Victoria, who never married; and Maud, who married King Haakon VII and became queen of Norway.

see in these circumstances a fortuitous push towards a norm of monarchical behaviour far closer to that of the present day: frequent public appearances but negligible influence on the running of governmental affairs.

Edward married in March 1863. Again Victoria respected Albert's wishes that Edward should marry young, and she was pleased with his chosen bride, the Danish-born Alexandra of Schleswig-Holstein. Edward was singularly fortunate in his marriage, for he genuinely loved Alexandra and the feeling was reciprocated. There is a certain paradox in his happy family life in view of his notorious and lifelong pursuit of pretty women. But there can be no doubt that he was extremely fond of Alexandra and adored his children, and likewise Alexandra was devoted to her husband and children. Whether she ever knew the full extent of her husband's unfaithfulness is not known. Perhaps she was mercifully naïve, or simply tolerant. Her feelings may well have been summed up in her words written after Edward's death: 'After all, he loved me the best.' There is no doubt also that the couple, despite the obvious difficulties and differences, brought up their children in a more relaxed and warm family atmosphere than had been provided for Edward by the stern combination of Victoria and Albert.

Alexandra, daughter of Prince Christian who later succeeded to the Danish crown, had been one of several prospective marriage-partners considered by Victoria and Albert. The Prince of Wales had met the seventeen-year-old girl in September 1861 at Speyer Cathedral and found Alexandra pleasant and attractive, though it was by no means a case of love at first sight. Edward's elder sister, Vicky, now married to Frederick of Prussia, the future Kaiser Frederick III, strongly supported Alexandra's candidature. She called her the most fascinating creature in the world and declared herself quite enchanted after meeting her. She wrote also: 'I own it gives me a feeling of great sadness when I think of that sweet, lovely flower – young and beautiful – that even makes my heart beat when I look at her – which would make most men fire and flames – not even producing an impression enough to last from Baden to England. . . . Bertie may look far before he finds another like her.'

Gradually, though, Bertie's affection grew, and he proposed to her a year after their first meeting and was at once accepted. 'I frankly avow to you', he wrote to his mother, 'that I did not think it possible to love a person as I do her. She is so kind and good.' He wrote also, 'I only feared that I was not worthy of her.'

Queen Victoria, though charmed by Alexandra, had some reservations on political grounds. Denmark and Prussia had long disputed the Danish-held territory of Schleswig-Holstein, and Victoria was anxious that her son's marriage should not involve Britain in the dispute. Alexandra was able to allay the Queen's fears completely, and Victoria wrote in her diary, 'How beloved Albert would have loved her.' In April 1863, one month after the wedding, the Queen took the young couple to Albert's mausoleum at Frogmore and, after a prayer, announced: 'He gives you his blessing.'

In view of the Queen's continued mourning for Albert, the wedding itself was bound to be rather a quiet affair. Edward and 'Alex', as the Princess was always known, were married in St George's Chapel at Windsor, and the Queen took no part in the procession, nor did she sit in the Chapel.

Edward and Alexandra produced six children in the course of the next eight years. The first was Albert Victor, Duke of Clarence, who was born in 1864. The following year George, later King George V, was born. There was also three rather plain daughters: Louise, born in 1867; Victoria, born a year later; and Maud, born the year after that. The last child, Alexander, was born in 1871 but lived only a few hours.

Alexandra had considerable grace and charm, and she inspired affection in those who knew her. Her unpunctuality was notorious. She was even late on the coronation day of her husband, and it is recorded that the King stormed to her room that morning saying, 'Hurry up, my dear, or you won't be crowned queen.' She was afflicted with a slight deafness which became worse as she grew older. In later years it became difficult for her to hear conversation, and in spite of her tact and smiles she became increasingly withdrawn from the social life which her husband so enjoyed at Marlborough House and Sandringham. Alexandra frequently wore a choker of jewels to hide a blemish on her neck, and such chokers quickly became

Opposite Edward, Prince of Wales and Alexandra with two of their six children, Albert Victor, Duke of Clarence and Princess Louise. A painting by Von Angeli. Edward and Alexandra remained devoted to their family despite the problems they faced from Edward's lifelong pursuit of beautiful women.

A page from the Diamond Jubilee edition of the *Illustrated London News* showing the development of transport and pioneers in the field, during Queen Victoria's reign.

the height of fashion among many Edwardian society ladies.

By the late 1860s the fortunes of the British monarchy had reached a low ebb. Even such public figures as Charles Dilke and Joseph Chamberlain were openly discussing the possibilities of a republic. To some extent, the unpopularity of the monarchy can be laid at the door of Queen Victoria. Her long seclusion and stern refusal to perform more than the minimum of public functions attracted many critics. Also, the prestige of the monarchy suffered considerably from

the activities of the Prince of Wales. Scandal was never far from the Prince, nor from the circles in which he liked to mix, and twice he was obliged to give evidence in a court of law. The first occasion was in 1871 when a member of Parliament, Sir Charles Mordaunt, brought a divorce petition against his wife for adultery with two of Edward's friends. Lady Mordaunt signed a confession admitting adultery not merely with the Prince's friends but with the Prince himself. Edward, summoned to the witness box on 23 February, denied the charge

Sandringham House in Norfolk was the favourite home of Edward and Alexandra. The main entrance, shown here, bears above it the coat of arms of the Prince and Princess of Wales.

A SARAH BERNHARDT

JULES BASTIEN=LEPAGE 1879

strongly, and he was not subjected to any cross-examination. But it transpired that he had on several occasions visited Lady Mordaunt while her husband was at the House of Commons. The scandal greatly shocked Alexandra and led to much open criticism of the Prince in the newspapers.

1871 was the year when monarchical fortunes reached their low point. From that year public sympathy grew perceptibly, due partly to the excesses of the Paris Commune in the wake of the Franco–Prussian War and partly to the wave of imperialist sentiment which swept the country during the last quarter of the century. The Queen's Golden and Diamond Jubilees in 1887 and 1897 provided magnificent occasions for honouring a queen who, by virtue of the length of her reign, was becoming a loved institution.

As powerful a force as any, drawing monarchy and subjects closer, occurred during the Prince of Wales's serious illness at the end of 1871. Typhoid fever, the dread disease which had carried away

Beautiful women played an important part in Edward's life. Sarah Bernhardt, the great French actress, had her name linked with that of the Prince of Wales during her first London visit in 1879. A portrait by Jules Bastien-Lepage.

26

Lillie Langtry, 'the Jersey Lily', was a favourite of the Prince of Wales. A painting by Sir Edward Poynter, R.A.

Albert, now threatened the life of his son. A wave of sympathy swept the nation, which watched tensely the frequent bulletins issued from Sandringham. The crisis inspired the following immortal lines, attributed sometimes to Alfred Austin:

> Across the wires the electric message came,
> He is not better, he is much the same.

The crisis point of the Prince's illness was reached on 14 December, the tenth anniversary of Albert's death. Edward, however, was spared, and the crisis brought something of a reconciliation between him and the Queen, who now realized how precious 'dear Bertie' really was to her.

Edward's reputation for loose living, both as Prince and as King, while by no means undeserved, has certainly suffered from exaggeration. Strict and often hypocritical standards of Victorian morality, the obvious contrast with the rectitude of Albert, and the

Alice Keppel, a discreet and intelligent woman, did valuable work in bringing the views of the Foreign Office to the King's notice.

sensation-seeking of the Press and of gossip-hungry society, all have combined to endow the Prince's behaviour with an aura of recklessness and dissipation out of proportion to reality. Late-night parties, hunting trips and occasional practical jokes at country house gatherings all brought reactions of horror from staid and sober citizens, and stern reproof from Queen Victoria. Edward's name was linked with innumerable women, among them Sarah Bernhardt, Lillie Langtry, Mrs Keppel, Miss Keyser, Hortense Schneider (a French actress), Lady Brooke and many more. Some certainly were mistresses, though others were simply companions. Edward never hid his interest in women, and society hostesses knew well that a successful evening could be assured only by putting Edward in the company of charming and amusing ladies. Otherwise a dull, bored expression would come over the royal visage, and an ominous drumming of the fingers would accompany a gruff 'Quite so, Quite so' to all attempts at conversation.

Edward had three principal mistresses. The first was Lillie Langtry, daughter of the Dean of Jersey and sometimes called 'the Jersey Lily'. At the age of twenty-one, she had married a young, prosperous widower, Edward Langtry. She was tall and strikingly good-looking with a magnificent figure. Lillie was ambitious to shine in London society, and Lord Ranelagh, who had a house in Jersey and who knew her, was only too willing to open the doors of London society for her. Edward Langtry took a house for her just off Knightsbridge, and from there Lillie was launched. She used her charms to good effect: Sir Alan Young, an Arctic explorer and a friend of the Prince, was so impressed that he arranged to introduce her to the Prince of Wales. The meeting was a great success, and within a month Lillie entered on her reign as mistress of the Prince, well-kept, well-housed and the envy of many aristocratic ladies who relieved their feelings by remarking on her vulgarity. Edward Langtry, having served Lillie's purpose by bringing her to London, became an alcoholic and finally a bankrupt. Meanwhile she became the most sought-after woman in town and was invited to innumerable receptions and weekend parties.

Lillie Langtry revelled in her position as the Prince's mistress. She was painted by Millais, Whistler and Edward Burne-Jones, and photographs of her were sold throughout the nation. The Prince often took her to Paris, and she was generally accepted as his mistress in a way unknown in England since the years of Charles II. Lillie realized that her relationship with the Prince was temporary, and she had ambitions to go on the stage. The Prince did everything he could to help in this ambition. He went to her début at the Haymarket Theatre in *She Stoops to Conquer*, introduced her to a leading actor-manager and took his friends to see her in her plays.

The second royal mistress was Frances Maynard, who was a member of the Court circle in her own right. She was twenty years younger than the Prince and had married Lord Brooke, who succeeded his father as Earl of Warwick. Frances, who was known as 'Daisy', was a considerable heiress, having inherited twenty thousand pounds a year from her grandfather. Queen Victoria at one time thought that she might be a good match for her son Leopold, but as neither Leopold nor Daisy liked each other the idea was dropped.

Daisy is one of the more interesting Edwardian beauties – intrepid, even reckless, with a mind of her own and considerable determination. Lord Brooke was an astonishingly tolerant husband, and she soon embarked on a series of love affairs, most notably with the Prince of Wales. She later wrote, after their first meeting: 'He was more than kind, and suddenly I saw him looking at me in a way all women understand. I knew I had won, so I asked him to tea.'

The liaison with Daisy lasted into the nineties, and Edward was clearly deeply in love with her. But Daisy, who had once spent a large part of her fortune on lavish entertainments, often given for the Prince, was having a change of heart. Increasingly she became influenced by the new doctrine of Socialism, and she began to bore the Prince with her lectures on this subject and by her attempts to influence him in this direction. Gradually the affair petered out, and the breach became final when the Prince was invited to dinner by the woman who was to remain his principal mistress until his death.

She was Alice Keppel, the daughter of an admiral and the wife of a brother of Lord Albemarle. The Keppels were a distinguished family, and they too were familiar in Court circles. Alice Keppel was twenty-nine when she met the Prince for the first time in February 1898. She was good-looking, clever and a good listener, and she greatly appealed to the Prince, who was by then fifty-seven years of age. Mrs Keppel was by all accounts the most expensive of Edward's mistresses, and he lavished a great deal of money on her. She also had a peculiar standing at Court and was tolerated even by Alexandra. The arrangement between King Edward VII and Alice was almost domestic, and Alexandra took a certain ironic pleasure in this. One day at Sandringham she burst out laughing when she saw her husband driving placidly in a carriage with Alice Keppel by his side as if they were a long-established couple, and it is well known that Alexandra permitted her to come and say goodbye to the King when he lay on his deathbed.

The Prince's love affairs were conducted with discretion, yet his morally dubious and socially wide circle of friends, his love of gambling and the turf, and his frequent sojourns in Europe's pleasure resorts brought a strong undercurrent of Press and parliamentary criticism and also constant anxiety to and admonition from his mother.

In 1891 the Prince was obliged once more to appear in court. The previous autumn he had stayed at Tranby Croft, the home of a wealthy ship-owner, for the St Leger race meeting. Baccarat was illegal, but this did not prevent the Prince and the other guests from playing each evening. When one of the guests, Sir William Gordon-Cumming, was discovered cheating, he was obliged to pledge himself never to play cards again. The pledge, signed by five witnesses, including the Prince, bound the participants to silence, but the story leaked out, and Sir William, in an unwise attempt to clear his name,

Frances, Countess of Warwick, in fancy dress as the Queen of Assyria. She was Edward's mistress for several years until she turned to Socialism and fell from favour.

'His Royal Highness the Prince of Wales and his American worshippers'. As Edward became the leader of a society that adored gambling and the turf, so an avid Press fed their readers with accounts and cartoons of his dubious behaviour.

brought his accusers to court. The Prince made repeated attempts to prevent the affair's being brought into open court, but in the end, in June 1891, he was obliged to give testimony against Gordon-Cumming. The verdict went against Sir William. In the aftermath of the trial, the Prince of Wales was vehemently denounced by Press and public, shocked that so leading a figure should have indulged in illegal gambling, and with army officers into the bargain. One newspaper referred to the Prince as a 'wastrel and whoremonger' as well as a gambler, and complained that it was not so much baccarat as 'the kind of life of which this was an illustration that was the cause of disgust'. Abroad, too, the monarchy fell into disrepute. 'The scandal cannot fail to add to the growing conviction that "royalty" is a burden to the British tax-payer for which he fails to receive any equivalent,' said the *New York Times*.

The Prince's reaction, as on previous occasions, was staunchly to justify his behaviour, to remain loyal to the friends so widely criticized and to refuse to modify his activities. But by the 1890s it might just be said that the Prince's foibles were becoming accepted by a society just itself beginning to escape from the strait-jacket of mid-Victorian morality. The Prince had long been a society leader, but now society was beginning to catch up.

Edward was clearly unfitted, by both temperament and talent, to be a dynamic ruler. On occasion he complained of the Queen's unwillingness to allow him access to official papers, but he never showed much inclination to undertake those royal functions relating to affairs of state. The Queen's lack of confidence in her eldest son's discretion was probably justified and had certainly been reinforced by the Prince's ill-considered and open espousal of the Danish cause during the war over Schleswig-Holstein in 1864; while that same year he had further shocked the Queen and the Cabinet by openly meeting the Italian rebel Garibaldi.

Prince Edward also showed little interest in domestic matters, and he rarely showed much enthusiasm for the Empire, in strong contrast both to his mother and to his second son, George, who later succeeded to the throne as George V.

In political matters Prince Edward's views on most issues were those of an unenlightened country squire. He did undertake various charity works and was mildly interested in the housing conditions of the working classes, yet he was, for example, opposed to female suffrage and thought it unwise to allow natives any part in the government of India.

Edward did show some interest in foreign policy, especially where Europe was concerned. And on several major issues he let his views be known to the government of the day. It can hardly be said, however,

Overleaf Street decorations for Edward's coronation. A watercolour painted by Charles E. Flower. The first coronation for over sixty years was naturally made much of by the people of London.

Below Edward leading in his horse Persimmon after winning his first Derby in 1896. His victory was enormously popular and the crowds gave him a tumultuous welcome when he led his horse in after the race. Edward's racing exploits won him not only the people's affection but also a measure of financial independence.

that he developed any consistent policy or attitude except a strong anti-German sentiment, which was enhanced by his dislike for his nephew the Kaiser.

From the late 1890s the Prince of Wales was, at last, permitted to undertake a few constitutional duties as Queen Victoria became increasingly infirm. Nonetheless, the Queen's death brought to the throne an ageing king whose habits, attitudes, thoughts and outlook were too strongly established to be changed, and who was not prepared to allow the multitudinous if trivial duties of the sovereign to interfere with his rather gross pleasures.

Victoria's death, so long expected, came nevertheless as a profound shock to the nation. Most of her subjects could not remember a time when Queen Victoria had not been on the throne, and there was a general awareness that Britain was entering on a new and difficult period in her history. Industrial and commercial supremacy was now being challenged by the United States of America and by Germany, and the German programme of naval building was an even more immediate threat to Britain's worldwide position.

The Boer War, which broke out in 1899, revealed both Britain's isolation and grave defects in her military organization. The early years of the century were to see British efforts to end her isolation by fostering ties abroad. And Edward, who, in a social sense, had never stood clear of European entanglements, was well fitted to preside over the transition.

For a few months after his accession, Edward VII did make some attempts to engross himself in constitutional matters. But he soon gave up and thereafter organized his life largely around his social occasions. Normally, he spent Christmas and the New Year at Sandringham, and one or two days in January shooting with friends on their estates. At the end of January he came to London to open Parliament and in February entertained at Buckingham Palace, frequently going out to dinner, to the theatre and to supper parties. By the beginning of spring he was in Paris, and then on to Biarritz for a few weeks, where Mrs Keppel would join him. Then followed a cruise for a month in the royal yacht *Victoria and Albert*, generally in the Mediterranean. He then returned to England in the early summer to preside over what was then 'the season'. In June he went to Windsor Castle for the Ascot races, and later would spend perhaps a few days in some provincial town before going on to the Goodwood races and to enjoy the hospitality of the Duke of Richmond. In August he went to Cowes for the yachting and then left for Marienbad in Bohemia, mainly for health and for social reasons. Returning from Marienbad, he would spend a few days at Buckingham Palace and then go on to the Doncaster races. And in the autumn he was at Balmoral for the grouse-shooting and deer-stalking. He then came down in the royal train to attend the autumn race meeting at Newmarket and in December was back at Sandringham for a week before returning to London for a fortnight's round of festivities, with visits to the theatre and to his friends.

Edward exerted himself little in matters of state. As mentioned

Opposite Edward is proclaimed King. An oil painting of the coronation by Lauritz Tuxen.

Above Sandringham, with its supply of pheasant and partridge, provided Edward with a regular opportunity to indulge his passion for shooting.

Left The King and Queen were great patrons of the arts. They are portrayed in their opera box on this contemporary music cover.

already, domestic policies and imperial matters bored him. But there was one major exception. Partly from family connections, partly from his love of European travel and partly from his own good-natured diplomatic qualities, he maintained a genuine interest in foreign affairs. It so happened that the King's own predilections were pro-French and anti-German, and these were the directions in which British political affinities were moving. Hence the King, through his family contacts and as representative of Britain, could usefully further the foreign policies of British governments, and Edward is especially remembered for his cementing of the *entente cordiale* with France.

The opening years of the twentieth century saw determined efforts by the British to end the 'splendid isolation' which now seemed less and less splendid. In 1902 Britain had broken a long tradition of avoiding formal political entanglements by entering into a limited alliance with Japan, which was then a rising Far Eastern power. In Europe, too, Britain was searching for friends if not allies. The Boer War had shown vividly both Britain's isolation and her military weakness, and German strength and ambitions were now threatening both France and Britain. Anti-British sentiment was strong in France. To ancient conflicts had been added recent colonial squabbles.

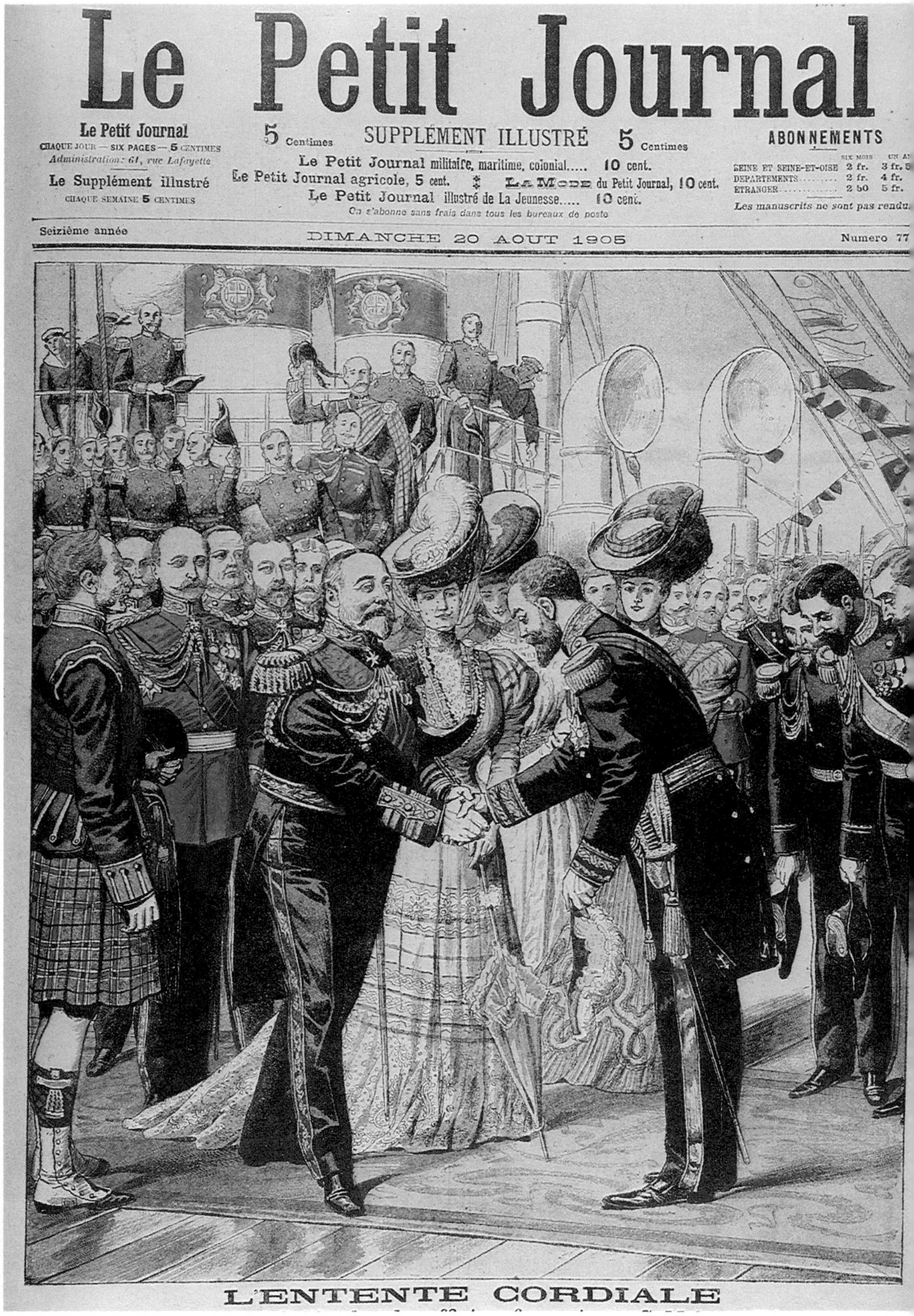

Le Petit Journal

Le Petit Journal
CHAQUE JOUR — SIX PAGES — 5 CENTIMES
Administration : 61, rue Lafayette

Le Supplément illustré
CHAQUE SEMAINE 5 CENTIMES

5 Centimes   SUPPLÉMENT ILLUSTRÉ   5 Centimes

Le Petit Journal militaire, maritime, colonial..... 10 cent.
Le Petit Journal agricole, 5 cent.   ‡   LA MODE du Petit Journal, 10 cent.
Le Petit Journal illustré de La Jeunesse..... 10 cent.
On s'abonne sans frais dans tous les bureaux de poste

ABONNEMENTS
SIX MOIS   UN AN
SEINE ET SEINE-ET-OISE   2 fr.   3 fr.
DEPARTEMENTS.........   2 fr.   4 fr.
ETRANGER.............   2 50   5 fr.

Les manuscrits ne sont pas rendus

Seizième année   DIMANCHE 20 AOUT 1905   Numero 77

L'ENTENTE CORDIALE

The *entente cordiale*: Edward welcomes the French fleet to British shores in 1905. The King had a strong interest in foreign affairs and was committed to the cause of Anglo-French friendship.

Nonetheless, French and British statesmen moved cautiously towards an understanding.

In the midst of intense diplomatic manœuvrings, the King prepared for himself an itinerary for a European tour which was to include a visit to France. The royal entourage arrived at Bois de Boulogne station on 1 May 1903 to be met not only by the French President but by cries of '*Vivent les Boers!*' from the hostile Parisians. Edward, who could be genial and charming when he wished, behaved with perfect tact and impeccable aplomb. His evident regard for France damped

anti-British feeling, and when, on 4 May, the King departed, it was to the cries of '*Vive Edouard! Vive notre roi!*' from the crowds.

But domestic matters soon closed in upon an unwilling monarch. Late in 1905 Balfour, the Conservative leader, whom Edward disliked and who in turn probably found Edward's philistine tastes of little appeal, resigned, and in the subsequent General Election in January 1906 the Liberals swept to an unprecedented landslide victory. The new government was radical and reformist and uncongenial to the King. The moving spirits behind its domestic reforms were the fiery Welsh Chancellor of the Exchequer, Lloyd George, and the young Winston Churchill, who went from the Board of Trade to the Home Office in 1910. Balfour, appalled at the prospect of such a powerful Liberal government, had taken comfort from the entrenched Tory majority in the House of Lords, still a body with powers in theory equal to those of the House of Commons. The stage was set, therefore, for a confrontation between Lords and Commons.

The spark to ignite the tinder was provided by Lloyd George's famous 'People's Budget' introduced in April 1909. Traditionally, finance bills passed in the Commons were unopposed by the House of Lords, but this Budget was different. Under the cloak of a finance bill, claimed the diehard Tories, the Liberals were introducing radical and disastrous political measures. In order to pay for such measures, such

David Lloyd George, the fiery Liberal politician who launched a crusade against property and poverty with his radical People's Budget of 1909, a campaign which the King sought to restrain.

as old age pensions, national insurance and enhanced military expenditure, a series of unpleasant taxes on the rich were to be levied. The level of income taxes and death duties was increased. Worse was the introduction of a super-tax levied at the rate of sixpence in the pound on incomes above five thousand pounds a year. But worst of all was a new land tax to tax the property-owner on increases in the site value of land (that is, where greater value was the result not of individual but of community enterprise). Such a budget was a direct challenge to the Conservatives. It remained to be seen whether 'Mr Balfour's Poodle', the House of Lords, would bite as well as bark.

Bite it did. In November 1909 a tense House of Lords, filled with many diehard peers, many of whom were making their very first appearance at Westminster, threw out the budget by 350 votes to a mere seventy-five. Asquith, the Liberal leader, at once asked the King to dissolve Parliament, and a new General Election took place in January 1910. Once more the Liberals were returned to power, but they had lost seats, and the government's majority now depended on the support of the minority parties – the Labour members and, most important, the Irish Nationalists.

Throughout the 1909 crisis the King's position had been an uncomfortable one. The constitutional right of the Lords to throw out the Budget had been by no means clear (the experts were divided),

Cartoons showing public concern about the 1909 People's Budget. The Budget saw the climax of a dispute that had been raging for two years between the House of Lords and the Commons. The King intervened when the Liberal government tabled legislation to curb the power of the Lords who had rejected the Budget, the first time this had happened for over a hundred years.

Above The peer has had his hereditary right to govern taken away and finds himself in the new and unwelcome position of having to listen to the voice of the people.

Above left Lloyd George is shown as the villainous pilot of an airship who misses his proper target and so hits the innocent people. The cartoon seeks to blacken Lloyd George's reputation by showing him as a German at a time of vicious pre-war anti-German public sentiment.

and the constitutional position of the King was likewise uncertain. Edward's own sympathies were largely with the opponents of the Budget. He deplored what he viewed as Liberal attempts to inflame 'the passions of working and lower orders against people who happened to be owners of property'.

The new Parliament offered little prospect of a break in the deadlock. The Irish Nationalists were determined to press for a Parliament Act to reform the House of Lords, for only by abolishing the Lords' legislative veto could they hope to secure a Home Rule Bill. Balfour was equally determined to oppose the Budget once more in the Commons. Thus, in order to get his Budget through the Commons, Asquith was obliged to propose the reform of the House of Lords. But, of course, it seemed a near certainty that the Lords would throw out such a measure, and the constitutional deadlock would be complete.

Various solutions were in the air. One was a referendum on the constitutional issue (supported strongly by Knollys, the King's Private Secretary). But the most obvious way out was if the King could be persuaded to guarantee the creation of enough Liberal peers to force through a Parliament Bill in case of rejection. Such a measure was, of course, intensely distasteful to the King, and he refused to give Asquith any such guarantee, at any rate until another General Election had been fought specifically on this constitutional issue.

In April 1910 the government presented the Commons with both its Budget and its Parliament Bill. The latter substituted for the Lords' veto a mere two-year delaying power, while the Lords could not even delay money bills at all. The Bill also reduced the period between General Elections from seven years to five. Asquith, though he had obtained no guarantee that the King would create sufficient Liberal peers, informed the Commons that he would, if the legislation were blocked, 'tender advice to the Crown as to the steps which will have to be taken if that policy is to receive statutory effect in this Parliament'. The Irish Nationalists, convinced now that Asquith would take necessary steps to reform the Lords, thereupon allowed the passage of the Budget. The Lords, realizing that the recent election had given the government a mandate, also passed the Budget. The stage was now clear for the constitutional struggle over reforming the Upper House.

The issues were complex. Asquith was determined to push through his legislation during the existing Parliament; the Liberals, after all, had just won a General Election. Yet Edward had already refused to give a pledge to create Liberal peers until another General Election had been held. It seemed inevitably as though the King would be drawn into a major constitutional dispute. Rumours of abdication, even of the end of the monarchy itself, were in the air. Then, at the height of the crisis, the King's health deteriorated suddenly. On the afternoon of 6 May he collapsed and just before midnight was dead. Britain had a new king.

Edward VII's death stunned the British public, for the majority of people were completely unaware that the sovereign's health was

The pre-war Suffragette movement had begun to take an increasingly militant position. With the outbreak of war in August 1914 they patriotically curtailed their campaign and turned to help the country.

anything but robust. Yet in fact his death had long been foreshadowed by increasingly frequent bouts of illness. From at least 1906 his health had been perceptibly in decline, minor ailments (such as a bad fall aboard the yacht of Sir Thomas Lipton) being accompanied by far more insidious, and ultimately fatal, bronchial attacks. It is an unpleasant fact that each of the four British kings who have died during the present century have had their deaths accelerated by excessive smoking. For much of his life Edward smoked several enormous cigars and twenty cigarettes *before breakfast*, rarely took strenuous exercise and ate gargantuan meals. By the time he entered upon middle age his waist measured forty-eight inches, the same as his chest.

By 1909 the King was seriously ill. Uncontrollable coughing fits and an increasingly gruff voice were outward manifestations of the illness while, at the same time, the King became increasingly irritable and subject to periods of melancholy. Early in 1909, while on a visit to Berlin, he was seized by a choking fit so violent that the Princess of Pless thought, 'My God he is dying. Oh, why not in his own country!' On that same visit a German official had noted: 'The King of England is so stout that he completely loses his breath when he has to climb upstairs,' and added, 'He eats . . . and smokes enormously.'

In April 1910 Edward visited Biarritz for the last time. Although the resort improved his spirits, as it invariably did, his return to England was quickly followed by a relapse. On 2 May a particularly severe bronchial attack left the King exhausted, though he still insisted on carrying out certain of his duties. On 5 May he gave an official audience, his last, to a visitor from Australia. That day, amid growing concern, his hastily summoned family gathered around him. The King remained optimistic, maintaining, 'I shall be about again in a day', but that evening his doctors issued a bulletin saying that 'his condition causes some anxiety.'

The following day, 6 May, the King rose as usual and received his friend Sir Ernest Cassel. Cassel left suspecting that this visit was to be his last. That afternoon Edward suddenly collapsed and suffered a series of heart attacks. As the King lay dying, his family and closest friends, Alice Keppel among them, said farewell to their sovereign. Scarcely able to breathe, Edward still insisted that he 'would fight it'. But at 11.45 pm the fight was over; the King had fallen into a coma, and his life slipped finally away.

The King lay in state in Westminster Hall, and a quarter of a million people filed past the coffin. Lord Morley wrote: 'The feeling of grief and the sense of personal loss throughout the country . . . is extraordinary. It is in a way deeper and keener than when Queen Victoria died.' Despite his faults (and many of his errant ways were, of course, totally unknown to most British people), Edward VII was an immensely popular monarch. About his throne had settled an atmosphere of genial good nature and glittering ceremonial qualities so long lacking at Britain's royal Court. Edward's resplendent funeral on 20 May, attended by many reigning sovereigns, their own races so nearly run, was an apt final tribute to a colourful and benevolent king.

A cartoon of a Suffragette and her children shown invading an Englishman in the sacred privacy of his home.

CHAPTER TWO

George v

The future King George v was born on 3 June 1865, the second son of the Prince and Princess of Wales. His parents decided to christen him George Frederick, though Queen Victoria, who disapproved of most things, disapproved of these names. She wrote:

I fear I cannot admire the names you propose to give the baby. I had hoped for some final name. Frederick is, however, the best of the two, and I hope you will call him so. George only came in with the Hanoverian family. However, if the child grows up good and wise I shall not mind what his name is. Of course you will add Albert at the end, like your brothers, as you know we settled long ago that all Papa's male descendants should bear that name to mark that line, just as I wish all the girls to have Victoria after theirs. I lay great stress on this; and it is done in a great many families.

The Prince of Wales would not change the name of his son, but he replied to his mother: 'We are sorry to hear that you do not like the names that we propose to give our little boy, but they are names that we like and have decided on for some time.'

As we have seen already, family life was one of the few Victorian virtues Edward found acceptable. He was devoted to his children and loved to play with them, and they responded with affection not unmixed with awe. With their mother there was no such reserve. She was loving to the point of possessiveness and perhaps found in her children the reciprocal and unshared love which was so clearly lacking in her marriage.

Royal children are no more immune from the influence of parental attachment than any other children. Edward suffered from the sternness of his upbringing, and Alexandra's children from the retarded emotional development that may have come from a clinging mother figure. Young Prince George, particularly, spent a great deal of time with his mother. She read aloud to him every day a passage from the Bible, and throughout his life, following this example, George always read a passage from the scriptures. He would sit by his mother as the maid brushed her hair, telling her about the activities of the day, and she was always there to tuck him into bed and speak to him before he went to sleep. And as long as she lived she remained 'Motherdear' to George, he 'Georgie' to her.

George being the second son, the main attention was naturally given to the elder boy, Albert Victor. 'Eddy', as he was always

Opposite The benign and dutiful King George v, by Calkin.

43

known, was eighteen months older than George, and the two boys were inseparable in childhood.

When George was six, he and Eddy began their formal education in the hands of their tutor, the Reverend John Dalton. Dalton appears to have been a good choice; strict without being severe, he always had the interests of his royal charges very much at heart. Prince George formed a bond with Dalton which lasted until the latter's death in 1931. The education mapped out by the Prince of Wales had little of the austerity imposed by Albert. Nonetheless, the regime was rigorous. The two Princes rose at seven each morning and studied English and geography before breakfast. At eight came bible study or history. At nine algebra or Euclidean geometry. Then came an hour's break before more lessons, usually Latin or French, until lunch at two o'clock. The afternoons were given over to sporting activities (a major contrast with the Prince of Wales's upbringing), after which came tea, English, music and homework. The Princes went to bed at eight.

Both Princes must have been a disappointment to their tutor in terms of academic progress. George proved himself a reasonably alert, diligent and co-operative boy. He also demonstrated the honest and straightforward character which so marked his years of rule. Not that he was a paragon. Dalton's diary notes for the week ending 2 September 1876 that his eleven-year-old pupil 'has been much troubled by silly fretfulness and temper and general spirit of contradiction'. And for 30 December: 'Prince George wants application, steady application. Though he is not deficient in a wish to progress, still his sense of self-approbation is almost the only motive power in him. He has not nearly so high a sense of right and wrong for its own sake as his elder brother.'

This favourable reference to Eddy is something of a rarity, for the elder Prince was a constant source of anxiety to his tutor and to his parents. Although not without charm, Eddy was backward and apathetic to the point of being 'simple'. He could rarely rouse himself to show an interest in his studies, in sports, in hobbies, or indeed in anything until his later remarkable sexual appetite developed. As the boys grew up, Eddy was constantly in his younger brother's shadow, for George was always the one to shine in company, and Eddy came to depend completely on him for such stimulus and interest as he could evolve.

This was a problem. George was not, of course, expected to succeed to the throne, and the Prince of Wales thought that a naval career would be a suitable one for his younger son. For Prince Eddy, the prospective King, such a training did not seem desirable. Yet equally undesirable, for Eddy at any rate, seemed the separation of the brothers. Dalton argued strongly that Eddy should accompany George to the Royal Navy training-ship *Britannia*, for the elder Prince might then attain 'those habits of promptitude and method, of manliness and self-reliance, in which he is now somewhat deficient'. And he wrote also:

Difficult as the education of Prince Albert Victor is now, it would be doubly or trebly so if Prince George were to leave him. Prince George's

Opposite An idealized portrait by Lafayette of Princess Alexandra. 'Motherdear', as she was known to her family, was inseparable from her son George who hated going to sea because it meant leaving her.

lively presence is his mainstay and chief incentive to exertion; and to Prince George again, the presence of his elder brother is most wholesome as a check against that tendency to self-conceit which is apt at times to show itself in him. Away from his brother, there would be a great risk of his being made too much of and treated as a general favourite.

Queen Victoria again disapproved. For both Princes to enter the service was hazardous, and 'the very rough sort of life to which boys are exposed on board ship is the very thing not calculated to make a refined and amiable Prince, who in after years (if God spares him) is to ascend the throne.' But Victoria's arguments failed to hold sway, and two days after his twelfth birthday George passed his entrance examination into the Navy. Accompanied by Eddy and Dalton, he joined the *Britannia* in September. This started a naval career which lasted for fifteen years, which saw George progress from cadet to captain and which endowed the Prince with a love of simplicity, orderliness and punctuality which would remain with him for the rest of his life.

The young Princes had a cabin to themselves, but in most respects they were treated exactly the same as the two hundred other cadets. It was a tough life of bare boards and stiff hammocks. George recalled later:

It never did me any good to be a Prince, I can tell you, and many was the time I wished I hadn't been. It was a pretty tough place and, so far from making any allowances for our disadvantages, the other boys made a point of taking it out on us on the grounds that they'd never be able to do it later on. There was a lot of fighting among the other cadets, and the rule was that if challenged you had to accept. So they used to make me go up and challenge the bigger boys – I was awfully small then – and I'd get a hiding time and time again.

In July 1879, when Prince George was just fourteen, he passed out of the *Britannia*, and shortly he and Eddy embarked on a world cruise which lasted for nearly three years. The boys sailed in the HMS *Bacchante*, a fully rigged ship with auxiliary engines. To the complement of 450 officers and men were added the ubiquitous Dalton and other tutors in mathematics, navigation and French for the Princes. The Cabinet strongly opposed the hazard of sending both sons of the Prince of Wales on the same ship, but this time Queen Victoria approved. 'I entirely approve the plans for my grandsons' journey,' she wrote to Disraeli, the Prime Minister, 'which should never have been brought before the Cabinet.'

The *Bacchante* made three separate cruises with her royal crew-members. The first lasted nearly eight months and took them to the Mediterranean and the West Indies. The second was a brief trip in which the *Bacchante* sailed with the Channel Fleet in the Western Approaches. The third and longest cruise extended from September 1880 to August 1882 and took George and Eddy to South America, South Africa, Australia, Japan, China, Singapore and Egypt. George was treated as a normal cadet, while Eddy, who was not considered for a naval career, concentrated without conspicuous success on his studies.

Prince George (*right*) with his brother Albert Victor, both wearing midshipman's uniform. A portrait by Carl Sohn the younger in Sandringham House.

The Princes enjoyed shore leave from time to time, though the instructions from the Queen were that they were not to be treated with royal honours. However, they were received with great formality at the Mikado's Court in Japan, and there were also occasional visits to royal relatives. Towards the end of the world cruise they went to Athens, and there visited an uncle and aunt, King George and Queen Olga of Greece, who made a tremendous fuss of the boys. Young George wrote on departure: 'We had to say goodbye to darling Aunt Olga and cousins. We all cried very much; we had spent such a delightful time here.'

The voyages, although they did much to shape the character of the future sovereign, were uneventful. Certainly, though, George had the opportunity of visiting imperial domains and obtained from these journeys a deep interest in the Empire which lasted all his life. A brief scandal occurred during the Prince's visit to Barbados, when an erroneous newspaper report drew attention to tattoo marks on the royal nose. Alexandra wrote to George asking, 'How could you have that impudent snout tattooed? What an *object* you must look, and won't everybody stare at the ridiculous boy with an anchor on his nose!' But it soon transpired that George's love of naval traditions did not extend to a tattooed nose. The marks were probably dust or pollen.

George found the long separation from his beloved mother hard to bear. As he left for the long third cruise, he wrote: 'My darling Motherdear, I miss you so very much & felt so sorry when I had to say

Prince George spent much of his early life in various naval vessels. In 1891 he commanded the gunboat HMS *Thrush*, shown here on the right of Edward de Martino's painting of the Channel Squadron.

goodbye to you and sisters. . . . I felt so miserable yesterday saying goodbye. I shall think of you all going to Scotland tonight & I only wish we were going too. . . . *So goodbye darling Motherdear, dearest Papa & sisters.*'

In 1883 the brothers separated for the first time when George became a midshipman in HMS *Canada*. Eddy now stayed at home to prepare for Cambridge University. He missed the company of his younger brother greatly and defied all attempts to kindle any intellectual spark in the royal brain. George, on the other hand, made a success of his career. During his training at Portsmouth on HMS *Excellent* he was awarded first-class marks in gunnery, torpedo work and seamanship, and in 1885 became a lieutenant.

As George passed into adulthood, he showed no signs of the dissipation that had characterized so many of his ancestors (and which was only too apparent in Eddy). His main interests outside the Navy lay in stamp-collecting and in the odd game of polo or billiards, and he remained fervently attached to Alexandra. Indeed, the sentimentality expressed in letters between mother and son borders on the nauseous. In 1886 he wrote to her: 'I cannot tell you how much I miss you every minute of the day. . . . I felt so low at saying goodbye to you.' And in 1888 he wrote from Naples:

In about three weeks' time I shall be leaving here for beloved old England again, it seems too delightful to be true and then in about a month's time, I shall see your beloved lovely face once more. Oh! Won't I give it a great big kiss and shan't we have lots to tell one another darling Motherdear after having been separated for these long seven months.

At Christmas in 1889, Alexandra could still tell her twenty-four-year-old son: '*how* dreadfully I missed you for Xmas. There were all the tables [containing Christmas presents] excepting yrs. & there were all their cheery voices excepting the cheeriest of all & yr. bright little face with its turned-up snout oh I did miss it & really shed a little secret tear for my Georgie dear.'

By the late 1880s the question of marriage for the Princes was being widely discussed and Victoria was particularly anxious for her grandsons to marry. Eddy, whose career at Cambridge and subsequently in the Army was an unhappy one, was the most urgent problem. After a series of rejections, a deep love affair with Princess Hélène of Orléans resulted in an engagement being announced in August 1890. But religious difficulties, for Hélène was a Catholic, proved insuperable, and the engagement was broken off. At the end of the following year Prince Eddy, who by now had been created Duke of Clarence, announced his engagement to Princess Mary

('May') of Teck. At the time of this announcement George was at Sandringham recovering from typhoid fever which for a time had threatened his life. This illness had killed his grandfather thirty years before, and nearly killed the Prince of Wales in 1871. George pulled through, but suddenly death struck the royal family from an unexpected direction. On 7 January 1892 Eddy caught influenza; the fever turned to pneumonia, and in a week the heir presumptive was dead.

George was heartbroken at Eddy's death, and he wrote to Queen Victoria: 'I am sure no two brothers could have loved each other more than we did. Alas! it is only now that I have found out how deeply I did love him; & I remember with pain nearly every hard

The wedding of Prince George, now Duke of York, and Princess Mary in the Chapel Royal, at St James's Palace in 1893. The Duchess of Teck, the bride's mother, sits in the foreground to the right, and opposite her (holding a fan) is Queen Victoria.

word & little quarrel I ever had with him & I long to ask his forgiveness, but, alas, it is too late now!'

For Prince George, of course, the death of his brother meant a complete change in his position. He might now expect one day to inherit the crown, yet his life until now had been circumscribed largely by the confines of a ship and by the ties of his family. In May 1892 George became Duke of York, Earl of Inverness and Baron Killarney. The following month he took his seat in the House of Lords and began to grapple with the mysteries of Parliament and of the constitution. He was now twenty-seven and had been in the Navy since the age of twelve.

Somewhat strangely (though Henry VIII had provided an unfelicitous precedent) George now became engaged to Princess Mary. Queen Victoria was a strong advocate of the marriage, writing that 'May is a dear, charming girl, and so sensible and unfrivolous'.

May was the daughter of Franz, Duke of Teck, and Princess Mary Adelaide of Cambridge. On her mother's side she was a great-granddaughter of King George III. She was born on 26 May 1867 in the apartments which had been allotted to her parents in Kensington Palace. May had a carefree childhood. Her mother persuaded her cousin Queen Victoria to let them have the delightful White Lodge in Richmond Park for a rural retreat. Mary Adelaide had an income from the government, but her extravagance, and consequent indebtedness, was legendary. The household employed a large staff of servants, while Princess May in her early teens was always attended by at least two personal maids. She and her brothers were invited to the royal houses in Britain and often visited their innumerable royal relatives in Europe.

In 1883 the Tecks' creditors could no longer be held at bay, and the entire family moved themselves to Florence, there to run up more debts, make new social contacts and continue the life of impecunious luxury. At the time, there was a brilliant social life in Florence, and this world had much to offer sixteen-year-old May. She gained assurance and poise in the hectic social milieu, and she also gained a fine education, read widely and developed an appreciation for the arts.

After two years in Italy, the Tecks were back in England. The initiative for the return came probably from Queen Victoria, who was searching relentlessly for a suitable bride for Prince Eddy. And Victoria, too, probably had a hand in the financial arrangements which enabled the Tecks to reside once more in England.

George's engagement to May was announced in the spring of 1893, and the royal wedding took place in the Chapel Royal at St James's Palace on 6 July. Neither of the couple found it easy to express emotions or affection. George was somewhat stern and unbending, while the Empress of Germany, his aunt and eldest child of Victoria and Albert, wrote of May that, 'All her thoughts and views seem to me rather banal and conventional.' It was probably more duty than love which first prompted George to seek Mary's hand, but by the time of the wedding there is no doubt that a sincere attachment had grown between them. Shortly before the wedding George had written

Queen Alexandra with her grandchildren, Prince Edward, Prince Albert (*left*) and Princess Mary. Alexandra lived in the main house at Sandringham after the death of Edward so that she would be near George and his young family.

to May: 'Thank God we both understand each other, & I think it really unnecessary for me to tell you how deep my love for you my darling is & I feel is growing stronger & stronger every time I see you; although I may appear shy and cold.'

After the wedding, a grand affair with numerous royal guests and tumultuous crowds on which the sun blazed from a cloudless sky, the Duke and Duchess of York spent their honeymoon at York Cottage in the grounds of Sandringham. 'Bachelor's House', as it was called until given as a wedding present to George and May, was in fact to be the main home for the couple for many years. George loved the small, cosy simplicity of the house, with its grounds overgrown with laurel and rhododendrons. For Princess May the attractions were less evident. Uncomfortable domestic arrangements and rural isolation were compounded by proximity to in-laws. Alexandra, who spent much time at Sandringham, and after her husband's death continued to occupy the main house for the remainder of her life, proved herself an interfering mother-in-law. She ordered furniture, decided how the rooms should be arranged and even how the small garden should be planted. Alexandra had never reconciled herself completely to losing George, and had written to him: 'Indeed it is sad to think we shall never be able to be together and travel in the same way – yet there is a bond of love between us, that of mother and child, which nothing can ever diminish or render less binding, and nobody can, or shall ever, come between me and my darling Georgie boy.'

George's married life was comfortable, happy and unblemished. His private life involved none of the moral taint which had marred that of his father, while in public he was correct and dignified without ever being scintillating. 'He believed in God, in the invincibility of the Royal Navy, and the essential rightness of whatever was British,' said his eldest son. George was, indeed, somewhat stiff to the point of dullness. He had a passion for the countryside, and an even greater passion for shooting anything that moved in it. He was a first-class shot, and shooting expeditions became his favourite pastime. On one occasion, remembered by his eldest son, a sumptuous shooting-party resulted in George's shooting over one thousand pheasants in a single day. Characteristically, the centrepiece of his 'Library' at York Cottage was not books but his collection of shotguns.

At times domestic life at York Cottage must have been a trial for Mary. The lack of company, the proximity of 'Motherdear', the tedious round of country gossip, George's failure to be interested in anything bordering on the intellectual or artistic, the incessant carnage from shooting parties – all must have necessitated a great deal of readjustment for the young bride. But readjust she did, and she made George a loyal, dependable and serene wife. Both as Princess and as Queen, Mary cut something of an awesome figure. Somewhat taller than George anyway, her headgear of toques added to her austere and forbidding appearance, and references became frequent to 'George and the Dragon'.

Mary was a better queen than mother. She enjoyed neither

The families of Edward VII and Tsar Nicholas II at Cowes in 1909. Queen Alexandra's sister was the Tsar's mother and Edward's sister was the Tsarina's mother. Back row: Prince Edward, Queen Alexandra, Princess Victoria and two daughters of the Tsar. Seated: Mary, Princess of Wales, Tsar Nicholas, Edward VII, the Tsarina, George, Duke of York and a daughter of the Tsar. The Tsarevich is sitting on the ground with another of his sisters. King George V was grief stricken when he heard of the murder of the Tsar and his family in 1918 and their fate haunted him for the rest of his life.

A coronation portrait of Queen Mary, 1918, by Sir William Llewellyn.

childbearing nor child-rearing and found it difficult to be on affectionate terms with her children. Yet she dutifully bore George six children: Edward, later Edward VIII (always known to his family as 'David'), was born in 1894; Albert 'Bertie', in 1895; Mary in 1897; Henry in 1900; George in 1902; and John in 1905. (Prince John, sadly, was soon found to be epileptic. He was brought up in isolation from the rest of the family on the Sandringham estate and died at the age of thirteen in 1919.) If the Duchess found motherhood uncongenial, George's attitude to his children was even less satisfactory. He became something of a tyrant, forever admonishing the Princes and failing utterly to recreate the friendly family atmosphere and affectionate relations with his children that had characterized his own upbringing.

Victoria's death in 1901 was a momentous event for the nation, and it was a momentous event, too, for George, who now became heir to the throne. Despite Edward VII's manifest failings, he was careful not to isolate his son from the affairs of statecraft as he had been isolated by the Queen. Official documents were opened to George, and gradually the heir to the throne gained poise and self-confidence in his dealings with ministers and government representatives. He also benefited considerably from the sagacity and experience of Sir Arthur Bigge, later Lord Stamfordham, who was his Private Secretary from 1901 till 1931. Later George acknowledged of Bigge: 'He taught me how to be a King.'

One of his first major duties in his new role was to embark upon an extended tour to Australia in March 1901. Before Edward's accession it had already been decided that the Duke and Duchess of York should open the very first parliament of the newly formed Commonwealth of Australia, and, despite the King's misgivings for the safety of his son, the royal couple duly undertook the planned engagement. In all, they visited Gibraltar, Malta, Aden, Ceylon, Singapore, Australia, New Zealand, Mauritius, Natal, the Cape of Good Hope, Canada and Newfoundland, and not only did the tour give the Duke confidence and experience of public speaking – he recorded in his diary that he had shaken hands 24,855 times – but he saw at first hand many of Britain's imperial possessions, and met the leaders of the self-governing Dominions.

George and Mary returned in November 1901, and the King then created his son Prince of Wales, writing to him:

In making you 'Prince of Wales and Earl of Chester', I am not only conferring on you ancient titles which I have borne upwards of fifty-nine years, but I wish to mark my appreciation of the admirable manner in which you carried out the arduous duties in the Colonies which I entrusted you with. I have but little doubt that they will bear good fruit in the future to knit the Colonies more than ever to the Mother Country. God bless you, my dear boy, & I know I can always count on your support and assistance in the heavy duties and responsible position I now occupy. Ever your devoted Papa, Edward R.I.

Overleaf The coronation luncheon held for George and Mary at the Guildhall, London, painted by Soloman J. Soloman.

During the early years of the present century, while an uneasy Britain struggled to end her isolation in the wake of the Boer War

humiliations and against the background of growing German strength, the Prince of Wales showed a greater interest in imperial matters than in European diplomacy. In October 1905 he and Princess Mary left for a six-month voyage to India. George was much impressed by the pomp and splendour of the maharajahs and by the magnificence of the ceremonies and processions in which he participated. Not surprisingly he found himself out of sympathy with the current agitation for more Indian representation in government, though he did note later, 'Evidently we are too much inclined to look upon them as a conquered & down-trodden race, & the Native, who is becoming more and more educated, realizes this & could not help noticing that the general bearing of the European towards the Native was to say the least unsympathetic. In fact not the same as that of superiors to inferiors at home.' Not surprisingly also, the Prince of Wales found time to kill large numbers of tigers and other animals which native beaters drove towards the royal gun-barrels.

Opposite The state progress of the royal coach through the streets of London for the coronation of King George V.

The last years of Edward's reign, as we have seen, were marked by a series of domestic crises precipitated by the great Liberal victory of 1906. George and Mary were in Burma when, in January, news of the landslide came through. 'I see that a great number of Labour members have been returned, which is a rather dangerous sign,' George wrote to his father, 'but I hope they are not all Socialists.'

The new Liberal government was reformist. Old age pensions, national insurance, the People's Budget, the Parliament Act and other controversial issues, such as female suffrage, strikes and Irish Home Rule dominated the domestic front until the events of 1914 turned men's gaze in other directions.

An abundance of memorabilia was produced for the coronation of George V. *Right* the front and back of a coronation mug.

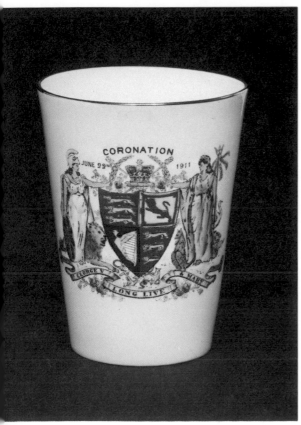

When King Edward VII died on 6 May 1910, George noted in his diary: 'At 11.45 beloved Papa passed peacefully away & I have lost my best friend & the best of fathers. I never had a [cross] word with him in his life. I am heartbroken & overwhelmed with grief, but God will help me in my great responsibilities & darling May will be my comfort as she has always been.' The funeral of the late King and the coronation of George V a year later were to be the last great foregatherings of European royalty. The Kaiser of Germany, the kings of Denmark, Portugal, Spain, Norway, Belgium, Greece and Bulgaria, the Archduke Franz Ferdinand of Austria and the Dowager Empress of Russia attended Edward's funeral. An age was passing, but it passed splendidly.

George's accession did not end the constitutional crisis over the People's Budget, but Asquith and Balfour did delay forcing the issue and agreed to hold an inter-party constitutional conference. Agreement could not be reached, however, the Conservatives being implacably opposed to Home Rule, while the Liberals depended on Irish Nationalist support in the House of Commons. In November 1910, therefore, Asquith asked the new King for a dissolution of Parliament, having obtained an undertaking from the sovereign that he would create sufficient Liberal peers to pass the Parliament Bill should the election result once more return the Liberals and should the Lords reject the measure. The King was unhappy about both the

The coronation Durbar held outside Delhi on
12 December 1911. The King and Queen, in
full coronation regalia, are seated on a
pavilion and flanked by Indian attendants
carrying peacock fans and golden maces. A
maharajah (*left*) pays homage to the King-
Emperor.

pledge and its secrecy, but fortunately he was not called upon to
honour it. The December election had again returned Asquith
(though still dependent on minority parties), and on 10 August the
King's promise to swamp the Lords was dramatically revealed on the
day of the debate in the Upper House. The news was sufficient to
persuade a majority of peers to allow the passage of the Parliament
Act. The King wrote: 'I am afraid it is impossible to pat the
Opposition on the back, but I am indeed grateful for what they have
done & saved me from a humiliation which I should never have
survived. If the creation had taken place, I should never have been the
same person again.'

Meanwhile George himself had proposed a coronation procession to be held in Delhi, and towards the end of 1911 the King and Queen left for India. The Durbar was held on 12 December 1911 and was a triumphant and spectacular affair, as the magnificently robed maharajahs paid homage to the King-Emperor. George was adamant that time be found for tiger-hunting. He killed thirty-one tigers, fourteen rhinos and four bears. Such was his evident relish for shooting these animals that the Secretary of State for India, Lord Crewe, wrote: 'It is a misfortune for a public personage to have any taste so strongly developed as the craze for shooting is in our beloved Ruler.'

On returning to England in February 1912, the King and Queen once more found the country in the midst of major domestic unrest. The Suffragettes were demanding the extension of the franchise to women, while the trades unions were growing in both strength and militancy at a time when living standards for many of the population were falling. More serious, however, from the viewpoint of politics and the constitution, was the Irish issue. Asquith introduced his Home Rule Bill in April 1912, and the Conservatives, bitter in the aftermath of their defeats over the Budget and the House of Lords, opposed the measure vehemently.

Resistance to the Home Rule Bill centred on Ulster. The Protestant population which owned the land, and most of the industry, had for long enjoyed a privileged position. Ulster Protestants were prepared to go to great lengths to avoid absorption into a Catholic Ireland largely independent of Westminster. History has seen many examples of religious hatred, often reinforced by economic motives, but there can have been few as intense as that which has divided, and still divides, Ulster from the rest of Ireland. Bonar Law, who had taken over the leadership of the Conservative Party, said: 'I can imagine no length of resistance to which Ulster will go which I shall not be ready to support, and which will not be supported by the overwhelming majority of the British people.'

The Ulstermen started to organize themselves, and many signed what was called 'The Ulster Covenant', pledging that, 'as loyal subjects of His Gracious Majesty King George V', they would use 'all means which may be found necessary to defeat the present conspiracy to set up a Home Rule Parliament in Ireland'. Inevitably, the Ulster movement involved the Crown.

Even as the Home Rule Bill steered its passage through Parliament, some influential Tories suggested that the King could refuse the Royal Assent to the Bill if it were passed. In 1913 the Ulster leader, Sir Edward Carson, proposed an amendment to exclude Ulster from the Bill, but it was defeated. The Bill was passed in the House of Commons, but it was then rejected, not surprisingly, by the House of Lords. Under the new Parliament Act, if the House of Commons passed the Bill again, it would automatically become law by the summer of 1914.

The mood of the House of Commons was such as it had not been since the struggles over the great Reform Bill of 1832. Even the common courtesies between members of opposing parties in the House were strained, and members who for years had been close friends now avoided each other. Almost openly the Ulster Protestants began to raise their own army. Dangerous conflicts of loyalties were arising: Field-Marshal Lord Roberts, a national hero of immense prestige, gave his support to the Ulstermen. Inevitably the Catholic Irish were forming their own army too.

The King was in an unenviable position. Most of the men whom he met socially were pro-Ulster. They argued that another election ought to be held on the one issue of Ireland, but Asquith had no intention of permitting this. Some of the King's friends told him that

he could dismiss the government, but Asquith warned the King that if he acted thus to a government which had a majority in the House of Commons, he would only make the Crown a 'football of contending factions'. Asquith thus concluded that, 'This is a constitutional catastrophe which it is the duty of every wise statesman to do the utmost in his power to avert.'

The King (*centre*) on a tiger-shoot in Nepal during the tour of India, 1912.

The rally to war: a patriotic recruitment poster depicting St George and the dragon, Britain's symbol of valour.

Opposite The heartache of war: 'The Departure' by Sir Frank Brangwyn, R.A.

By 1914 the danger of civil war in Ireland became greater day by day. In March Asquith made a gesture to the Ulstermen by offering to exclude the province from the measure for six years, to give time for the situation to settle. But both Bonar Law and Sir Edward Carson refused to accept this compromise.

And now occurred an even more dangerous development. If the Home Rule Bill became law and Ulster took to armed conflict, it would be the duty of the government to use the British Army to crush the rebellion. But many army officers decided that they would have no part in taking action against their fellow-countrymen in Ulster.

Towards the end of March 1914 Sir Arthur Paget, the commanding officer of the troops in Ireland, was summoned to London and ordered to take precautionary measures in Ulster. He returned to his headquarters and passed on the orders, but as a result most of the officers of the Cavalry Brigade resigned. For a time it seemed that the British Army might be in a state of mutiny within a few weeks.

The King then made a final effort to preserve peace. On his own initiative he arranged a meeting of the opposing parties at Buckingham Palace. In his opening address he said: 'For months we have watched with deep misgivings the course of events in Ireland. The trend has been surely and steadily towards an appeal to force, and today the cry of civil war is on the lips of the most responsible and sober-minded of my people.' The conference met on 21 July and ended in failure three days later.

The evening newspapers which, on 24 July, carried news of the failure of the conference, carried also the terms of the Austrian ultimatum to Serbia. In the memorable words of Winston Churchill: 'The parishes of Fermanagh and Tyrone faded back into the mists and squalls of Ireland, and a strange light began immediately, but by perceptible gradations, to fall and grow upon the map of Europe.'

Just as King Edward's death had intervened in 1910 when constitutional deadlock had seemed inevitable, now, with civil war in Ireland apparently so imminent, a new danger suddenly dwarfed the issue of Home Rule. On 4 August 1914 the King and Queen, accompanied by the Prince of Wales, stood on the balcony of Buckingham Palace to witness the cheering throngs below. Britain and her allies were now at war with the German Empire.

By mutual accord the Home Rule Act was allowed to pass but was to have no force for the duration of hostilities and would then operate only with adequate safeguards for Ulster. Thus a common threat imposed peace on warring factions.

Details of the deep-rooted origins of the war, which eventually ranged Britain, France and Russia against Germany and Austria–Hungary – the terrible battles of attrition in the trench warfare of the Western Front, the complex political manœuvrings that brought Lloyd George to the head of a coalition government at the end of 1916, and ultimate victory over Germany in 1918 – are far beyond discussion here. But it must be stressed that the war brought for George V not only the nightmare of being Head of State, locked in battle with the mighty German Empire; not only the natural anxiety

of any father whose sons were involved (for Bertie's ship took part in the battle of Jutland, though the authorities did their best to keep his brother David from danger in his frequent visits to regiments at the Front); but also the intensely personal horror of war against nations ruled by members of his own family. Moreover, Britain's very success ultimately helped destroy the old system of monarchy for ever. The Courts of Europe vanished in the mud and slaughter of the Somme and Passchendaele, just as surely as did so many of the troops who fought.

As Head of State, the King was naturally the focal point for the upsurge of patriotic fervour which swept the country in August 1914. Young men fought and died 'for King and Country'. The King himself was deeply moved by the cheering crowds, as he was by the sufferings his people were forced to undergo. Throughout the war he devoted himself tirelessly to his constitutional duties, which were now enhanced considerably by the conduct of war, and he took every opportunity to visit industrial areas, attend military parades and inspect the troops, confer decorations and visit the wounded in hospitals. He had even, at the instance of Lloyd George and to his later bitter regret, agreed to abstain from alcohol for the duration of war. 'I hate doing it but hope it will do good,' he had written. But in fact the royal example to the working man was followed by few others in high places, and the crusade, in Harold Nicolson's words, 'left His Majesty high and dry'.

The King also made five journeys to France, where he visited the trenches and saw at first hand the sufferings involved in this type of warfare. The King was even wounded, though ingloriously, on one of his expeditions to France: in October 1915 his horse fell and rolled on him fracturing his pelvis, and he was ever after subject to pain from the injury, which probably contributed towards his bad temper in subsequent years.

The King's popularity was undoubtedly increased by his readiness to appear on public occasions and to identify himself with the sufferings of his people. The Prince of Wales, too, by his eager visits to the front line and evident willingness to meet the common man, won immense public popularity which attached itself to the monarchy generally. Yet there were numerous criticisms of the monarchy, not simply from Socialists but oddly from those ultra-patriots who so despised things German that they stoned dachshunds in the streets and decried Mozart and Beethoven. Soon after the opening of hostilities, the King had been saddened to have to agree to the resignation of his brilliant cousin Prince Louis of Battenberg as First Sea Lord, as there had been a public outcry against the Prince's German birth and name. The following year a similar ignorant clamour brought the downfall of the German-educated Lord Haldane, despite his magnificent work in reorganizing the British Army.

Early in 1917 a campaign began to discredit the Royal Family for their own German background, for George ruled as head of 'the House of Saxe-Coburg and Gotha'. The issue became urgent, since

Spy cartoon of Sir Arthur Bigge, later Lord Stamfordham, Private Secretary to George V for thirty years.

Opposite The war touched everyone. Back at home women rallied to support the men at the Front. They were able for the first time to make a significant contribution to the war effort by making weapons.

the overthrow of the Russian imperial family in March had heralded a brief outburst of republicanism. H. G. Wells referred to the 'alien and uninspiring Court', to which the King's reaction, typically, was, 'I may be uninspiring but I'll be damned if I'm an alien.' Nonetheless, Lloyd George saw that there might be political advantages in a new royal name, and the King reluctantly conceded the necessity of a change. But to find an appropriate name was no easy matter. The College of Heralds came up with 'Wettin' and 'Wipper' – hardly names to provide a patriotic rallying cry. 'Fitzroy' and 'Tudor-Stewart' were among numerous other proposals, but eventually, and fortunately, Lord Stamfordham came up with the name of 'Windsor', which became the official royal name on 17 July 1917.

The armistice of 11 November 1918 brought peace at last. But four short years had wrought tremendous changes throughout society, though few could yet comprehend the magnitude of the forces. Britain was victorious, but from now on her weakened economy resulted in large-scale unemployment and widespread labour troubles. The Liberal Party was largely a spent force; Labour now appeared as the challenge to the Conservatives. The state had come to play a greatly enlarged role in many aspects of economic and social life. Above all, Britain, like other nations, had lost the flower of a generation. Much of the old stability and many of the former values were gone. A new spirit, active, hedonistic, less willing to acknowledge established customs, was abroad.

This new world, shorn of so many European royal Houses, where unfamiliar-sounding republics had replaced once mighty empires, George found increasingly difficult to understand. He shared with many of his subjects a nostalgic yearning for the lost world before 1914, with its self-assurance and stability. He was deeply disturbed by the sad fate of so many of his relatives overseas, especially by the brutal murder of his cousin Tsar Nicholas II and his family by the Bolshevik revolutionaries. Yet, as constitutional monarch, he had to wrestle in the aftermath of victory with the deep and often intractable problems which so beset the interwar years.

Ireland had been the major domestic issue before August 1914, and it proved so again after 1918. The savage repression of the Easter Rising of 1916, when sixteen leaders of the rebellion were executed, made it certain that the South would fight for Irish independence. And throughout 1919 and 1920 there raged a virtual civil war. The King tried hard to bring about a reconciliation between the factions and at great personal risk of assassination insisted on opening the new Ulster Parliament in Belfast in 1921. His speech on this occasion hinted at the solution ultimately adopted: Dominion status for Southern Ireland. The Cabinet was bitterly divided at the prospect of Irish independence, as indeed were the Southern Irish at the prospect of partition. Nonetheless, the Irish Free State came formally into existence in January 1922, and a new era, though not one of prolonged tranquillity, began for Ireland.

A sign of the new times appeared in January 1924 when Britain acquired its first Labour government. It is difficult today to realize the

Above 'Existence', one of Paul Nash's famous and evocative paintings showing the grim reality behind the promises of glory – waiting for days on end in the rat-infested trenches of France.

widespread dread and horror with which such an event was viewed. There were wild rumours of a Bolshevik takeover, and some felt that the King had a constitutional duty to thwart a Labour government. The election of December 1923 had failed to give the Conservatives, under Baldwin, a clear majority, and Baldwin was in consequence defeated by the combined votes of Liberal and Labour members when the House of Commons met the following January. The King, who had no wish to provoke a constitutional crisis, determined to send for Ramsay MacDonald as leader of the second biggest party. His record of the historic interview on 22 January is touching:

At 12.15 I held a Council, at which Mr Ramsay MacDonald was sworn as a member. I then asked him to form a Government, which he accepted to do. I had an hour's talk with him, he impressed me very much; he wishes to do the right thing. Today twenty-three years ago dear Grandmama died. I wonder what she would have thought of a Labour Government!

One of the King's new ministers, J. R. Clynes, has recorded his memories of his summons to the Palace:

King George sent for Mr MacDonald. Arthur Henderson, J. H. Thomas and myself accompanied our leader to Buckingham Palace to that fateful interview of which we had dreamed, when a British Sovereign should entrust the affairs of the Empire to the hands of the people's own representatives. As we stood waiting for His Majesty, amid the gold and crimson magnificence of the Palace, I could not help marvelling at the strange turn of Fortune's wheel, which had brought MacDonald, the starveling clerk, Thomas, the engine-driver, Henderson, the foundry labourer and Clynes, the mill-hand, to this pinnacle beside the man whose forebears had been kings for so many splendid generations. We were making history.

We were, perhaps, somewhat embarrassed, but the little, quiet man whom we addressed as 'Your Majesty' swiftly put us at our ease. He was

Right Three medals from the war years known to soldiers as 'Pip, Squeak and Wilfred', after the *Daily Mirror* cartoon characters – a dog, a penguin and a rabbit – drawn by A. B. Payne. From left to right, the 1914 Star, the British War Medal, the Victory Medal.

himself rather anxious; his was a great responsibility, and I have no doubt that he had read the wild statements of some of our extremists, and I think he wondered to what he was committing his people. The King first created MacDonald a Privy Councillor, and then spoke to us for some time. He gave us invaluable guidance from his deep experience, to help us in the difficult time before us, when we should become his principal Ministers. I had expected to find him unbending; instead he was kindness and sympathy itself. Before he gave us leave to go, he made an appeal to us that I have never forgotten: 'The immediate future of my people, and their whole happiness, is in your hands, gentlemen. They depend upon your prudence and sagacity.'

This was the beginning of a remarkable period, both for the King and for MacDonald and his colleagues. From the start there was complete confidence between the King and the Prime Minister. George also became on good terms with a number of Labour ministers, and particularly he enjoyed the earthy humour and informality of J. H. Thomas. The King wrote to his mother: 'I have

'The Cemetery, Etaples, 1919' by Sir John Lavery. The flower of Britain's youth was lost in the wholesale slaughter that occurred in the trenches.

The King followed events closely and made many visits to the battlefields of war-torn France. He is seen here with his son the Duke of York (second from left) inspecting a soldier's grave.

been making the acquaintance of all the Ministers in turn, and I must say they all seem to be very intelligent and they take things very seriously. They have different ideas to ours as they are all Socialists, but they ought to be given a chance and ought to be treated fairly.'

The minority Labour government lasted only until October, when Baldwin once more became Prime Minister.

The next major crisis was the General Strike, which started its nine-day course on 4 May 1926. During the strike the King showed himself a good deal more temperate than some of the strikers' opponents. 'Try living on their wages before you judge them,' was his reaction to a wealthy colliery-owner who called the miners 'a damned lot of revolutionaries', and he deplored the militant language of the Chancellor of the Exchequer, Winston Churchill. Above all, the King was relieved at the commonsense and absence of bloodshed which characterized the strike. He wrote later: 'Our old country can well be proud of itself, it shows what a wonderful people we are.'

By the mid-1920s the King's health was failing. Recurrent chest

The King chatting to a young worker in a Sunderland yard during a tour of the ship-yards and munitions workshops of the north-east coast of England. King George was the first monarch to fully develop the royal tour, which gave ordinary working men and women a chance of seeing their King.

ailments were now added to the periods of pain from his wartime injuries. In November 1928 he was struck by a chest abscess which brought him to the point of death. The Prince of Wales was hastily summoned from an East African safari. A letter from his brother was awaiting him in London:

My dear old David, since writing to you this evening I have seen Dawson. Papa's temperature has again gone up tonight which is a worry, but has not altered Papa's condition very materially as he is stronger physically. There is a lovely story going about which emanated from the East End that the reason of your rushing home is that in the event of anything happening to Papa I am going to bag the throne in your absence, just like the Middle Ages!! Ever yours, Bertie.

Lord Dawson, the King's principal physician, finally located the abscess on 12 December. He operated at once, and the King's life was saved. But George remained weak, subject always to renewed lung disorders. In the words of Elizabeth Longford: 'If he was permanently weakened by the accident of 1915, he was left with a fading sunset mellowness by his illness of 1928–9, often broken, however, by shafts of vivid petulance or indigo banks of boredom.'

Increasingly, the King devoted himself to his shooting expeditions at Sandringham and to his monumental stamp collection, as far as his

George v at the microphone making his first Christmas broadcast, from Sandringham, 1934. King George was the first British king to use the radio as a means of reaching vast numbers of his people.

constitutional duties permitted. In these declining years, he found solace in the company of his grandchildren, especially Elizabeth, whom he called 'Lilibet' and whom he adored. It has already been observed how, once his own children married, the King's attitude towards them had mellowed and softened. Princess Mary had married Viscount Lascelles, heir to the Earl of Harewood, in 1921. Early in 1923 Bertie had also married outside royalty, his bride being Lady Elizabeth Bowes-Lyon. At the time of the King's death, only Prince Edward remained a bachelor. The relations between the Prince of Wales and his father were frequently strained by the strong sense of disapproval felt by the King for his son's outlook, clothes and friends. The Prince wrote of his father: 'He disapproved of Soviet Russia, painted finger nails, women who smoked in public, cocktails, frivolous hats, American jazz and the growing habit of going away for weekends.' And he added: 'While I shared my father's mistrust of Communism, I couldn't see anything glaringly reprehensible about the others. Our differing views on these and related trends of my generation not unnaturally made for occasional misunderstandings between us.'

The King suffered a number of grievous personal losses in these years. In November 1925 his beloved mother, Queen Alexandra, died shortly before her eighty-first birthday, and the year 1931 brought a series of losses which further severed the King's links with his childhood and youth: in January his eldest sister, the Princess Royal, died; shortly afterwards, he lost his oldest friend and equerry, Sir Charles Cust; in March Lord Stamfordham, the King's Private Secretary, who for thirty-one years had guided George both as Prince of Wales and as King through his constitutional duties, died too; finally, in July, came the death of Canon Dalton, tutor to George and Eddy sixty years before.

1931 also marked the last major constitutional ordeal of the King's reign. In the summer of that year an unprecedented situation arose when, in the midst of a grave economic crisis, the Labour Cabinet split over the question of cuts in unemployment pay. MacDonald, the Labour leader, had no alternative but to offer the Cabinet's resignation, but the King, who liked and respected MacDonald and who had already taken soundings from the Liberals, suggested that MacDonald stay on as leader of a coalition National Government. The result was that MacDonald stayed on, with only a handful of Labour ministers, to run what was virtually a Conservative government. At the time the King's action in calling on MacDonald was much criticized as unconstitutional, especially by Labour supporters. It is now clear, however, that the King acted on the fullest advice from his ministers and that he did not overstep the bonds of his constitutional prerogative.

The King always retained his devotion to the Empire (his stamp collection, confined as it was to Britain and the Empire, was a practical symptom of this love). His reign saw the culmination of Empire, for the collapse of the enemy empires in 1918 had resulted in major new territorial acquisitions. But it saw also the beginnings of decline. Irish Nationalism had provided one major crack, while in India nationalist agitation led by Gandhi was steadily undermining British rule. When the King was obliged to receive Gandhi at Buckingham Palace in September 1931, his immediate reaction on hearing of the proposal was to roar: 'What! Have this rebel fakir in the Palace after he has been behind all these attacks on my loyal officers!' And he could not forebear to warn the Indian: 'Remember, Mr Gandhi, I won't have any attacks on my Empire.'

The White Dominions, too, were anxious to have a greater measure of independence, and in 1931 the Statute of Westminster redefined the relations between Dominions and Crown, and thus pointed the way towards Commonwealth rather than Empire.

The close of the King's reign brought the magnificent Silver Jubilee celebrations of 1935. Flags and decorations appeared in streets throughout the country. Jubilee tea-parties for children were held. And everywhere the King and Queen went they were met by cheering and flag-waving crowds. The King was deeply moved by his reception and, after one such event in London's East End, recorded: 'I'd no idea they felt like that about me. I am beginning to think they must like me for myself.' The climax was Jubilee Day itself, 6 May, just a few weeks before George's seventieth birthday, when he and the Queen drove to St Paul's Cathedral for a thanksgiving service. The King wrote in his diary: 'A never to be forgotten day, when we celebrated our Silver Jubilee. It was a glorious summer's day: 75 degrees in the shade. The greatest number of people in the streets that I have ever seen. The enthusiasm was most touching.' That evening he spoke on the radio to his subjects in his deep, comforting voice, already familiar to millions through the Christmas broadcasts he had pioneered since 1932:

At the close of this memorable day, I must speak to my people everywhere. How can I express what is in my heart? ... I can only say to you, my very, very dear people, that the Queen and I thank you from the depths of our hearts for all the loyalty – and may I say so? – the love, with which this day and always you have surrounded us. I dedicate myself anew to your service for all the years that may still be given me.

But only months were to be given him. Towards the end of the year the King became ill. On 3 December he was heartbroken to learn of the death of his favourite sister, Victoria, and he cancelled the State Opening of Parliament due for that day. Although he managed his final Christmas broadcast, he never again appeared in public. He fell ill once more on 15 January. The Prince of Wales was called to Sandringham by Queen Mary, and, surrounded by his wife and children, the King's life ebbed away on 20 January. 'The King's life is moving peacefully to its close,' was the famous bulletin issued by Lord Dawson at 9.25 pm. One of his last whispers had been: 'The Empire?' 'It's absolutely all right, Sir,' his Private Secretary replied. Just before midnight, King George v died. Queen Mary turned to her eldest son and kissed his hands. The King was dead. Long live the King.

Opposite The King as Field-Marshal: reviewing British regiments of which he was Colonel, on the occasion of his Silver Jubilee. A page from a Jubilee issue of the *Illustrated London News*.

CHAPTER THREE

Edward VIII

King Edward VIII's story is, inevitably, the story of his abdication, an event unique in the annals of the English constitution and one which brought to the throne yet another inexperienced and unprepared second son. No Prince of Wales had ever been so popular as Edward, none more evidently suited to the duties of kingship. Yet his rule lasted for less than eleven months. Suddenly and dramatically the crisis broke upon the unsuspecting public: the King would abdicate rather than yield the woman he loved.

In retrospect many threads of the 1936 crisis can be traced back much earlier, some, indeed, to the Prince's early childhood and upbringing. To raise the question of why Edward, in the final analysis, put personal happiness before duty is to raise the complex question of what the monarchy itself meant for him. There can be no doubt that the very informality and common touch which so endeared the Prince of Wales to the public were symptoms of an attitude towards the monarchy which, once Edward succeeded his father, led unwaveringly towards the tragedy of abdication.

Edward was born in 1894, in the fifty-seventh year of the reign of his great-grandmother, Queen Victoria. On 23 June of that year, the future King George V wrote in his diary: 'At ten a sweet little boy was born and weighed 8 lb.' His full names were 'Edward Albert Christian George Andrew Patrick David'. From the outset all attention was focused on this eldest child 'David', a singularly attractive boy with fair hair and deep blue eyes. Edward's beauty as a child and perpetual youthfulness as a man earned him the tags 'Prince Charming' and later 'Peter Pan'. Duff Cooper, watching the State Opening of Parliament when Edward was in his mid-teens, wrote of 'the King and Queen sitting on their thrones ... the Prince of Wales on a smaller throne in the robes of the Garter, looking most like a fairy prince, his pink face and golden hair rising out of ermine, beautiful as an angel'.

Even as a baby Edward was the favourite. The nurse to the royal infants used to neglect poor Bertie and feed him so irregularly that he early developed gastric disorders which remained with him for the rest of his life. This nurse even went so far as to pinch Edward's arm when formally presenting the babies to their parents in the evenings, so that he would cry on being transferred to the arms of his mother.

As time passed and as the Princes went beyond babyhood to

Opposite Edward, Prince of Wales, by John St Helier Lander.

Prince Edward (standing) with his great-grandmother Queen Victoria and his younger brothers and sister Princess Victoria, Prince Albert (sitting) and Prince Henry in the Queen's arms.

boyhood and to adolescence, relations between parents and children – especially between Edward and his father – were strained. Just why King George, whose relations with his own parents had been so good and who always seemed at ease with other people's children, should have found dealing with his own offspring so difficult, is a puzzle. In a perceptive passage Harold Nicolson has written:

He may have felt that, bred as they had been in the artificial atmosphere of a Court, they needed a discipline, the rigours of which he alone was in a position to apply. He may have exaggerated the contrast between the remembered ordeals of his own youthful training and what seemed to him the softer slackness of a degenerate age. He may have sought – sometimes by irritated disapproval, more often by vociferous chaff – to check in them what he vaguely recognized as the revolt of post-war youth against the standards and conventions in which he had himself been nurtured. He may even have regarded his immediate family as a ship's company of whom he was the master and the martinet, and have adopted towards them a boisterous manner which, however suited to the quarter-deck, appeared intimidating when resounding amid the chandeliers and tapestries of palatial saloons. Although sensitive, he did not always exercise imaginative insight into the sensibility of others. In seeking to instil into his children his own ideals of duty and obedience, he was frequently pragmatic and sometimes harsh.

Possibly also George was haunted by the spectre of the debauched Prince Regent which had so dominated his own father's upbringing. Certainly, once his children married, George's attitude towards them softened and warmed considerably, and it may well be that he saw in the sanctity of marriage a sufficient safeguard against the dread moral dangers surrounding unattached youth. And Edward never married in his father's lifetime.

King George early decided that there was no better education for princes than that which he had himself experienced. They were to be educated by private tutors at home at York Cottage until the time came for them to enter the Royal Navy. So, when Edward was approaching eight and Albert was six, a Mr Henry Hansell, a graduate of Oxford who also had considerable athletic prowess, was engaged as tutor for the Princes. Hansell himself was not at all convinced that such isolated tuition away from the society of other boys was the best means of educating the Princes. But when the subject of schooling was mooted, George said simply: 'My brother and I never went to a preparatory school; the Navy will teach David all that he needs to know.'

Hansell did his best to make the study room at York Cottage resemble a classroom. School desks were imported, a blackboard was fixed, and a strict timetable was laid down. Thus the Princes were woken at seven and by seven-thirty were at their desks for three-quarters of an hour of 'homework' before breakfast. Then at nine o'clock came lessons until lunchtime, a walk or games after lunch, more lessons until tea, the last meal of the day, then more lessons until about six o'clock.

The children saw little of their parents, although they always saw their mother during her rest period at six-thirty each evening. But of course the calls of official duties in London, the calls of the hunting season in Scotland and the lengthy voyages overseas which George and Mary, as Prince and Princess of Wales, undertook after the death of Queen Victoria, meant that the parental figures were somewhat remote during the most formative years of the Princes' childhood.

George was intensely critical of his children, rarely spoke kindly to them and was grudging in praise. He constantly 'chaffed' them about their studies, appearance and conversation. Graver matters would bring a summons to 'the Library' and a severe scolding. Edward, the usual recipient of such summonses, wrote subsequently that: 'The Library became for us the seat of parental authority, the place of admonition and reproof.'

Edward entered the Royal Navy College at Osborne in May 1907, when nearly thirteen years of age. There he began four years of onshore training preparatory to going to sea. As might be expected, the sudden thrust into the company of other boys brought immense and sometimes painful problems of readjustment. An early such episode occurred when some of the young cadets decided that his golden locks would look better dyed with red ink. Nonetheless, he soon settled down well, though without ever excelling in the mathematical and other nautical studies which were part and parcel

Prince Edward (*left*) and Prince Albert with their tutor Mr Hansell, 1911. Mr Hansell thought the young princes should attend a school but King George would not hear of it.

Above King George presents Edward, Prince of Wales, to the people at the investiture in Caernarvon Castle. The Prince was greatly embarrassed by his 'fancy dress' but Queen Mary thought he 'looked charming'.

Left Prince Edward as a naval cadet. He and his brother went first to Osborne, a preparatory college, and then to Dartmouth. King George had had a tough upbringing in the Navy and believed implicitly that there was no better training for his sons.

of the training of a naval officer. After two years at Osborne (by which time Bertie too had entered), Edward transferred for his final training period to Dartmouth Naval College on the south Devon coast.

The death of Edward VII in 1910 brought the young Prince within one step of the throne. Automatically he became Duke of Cornwall, with hereditary estates in the west of England and in London. Although Edward continued his naval training, he was conscious of a changed attitude towards him from his fellow cadets. On his sixteenth birthday the King created his son Prince of Wales, and, before the coronation a year later, Edward was made a Knight of the Garter so that he might wear the robes of that ancient order at the ceremony, for he was not yet of age to wear the robes of a peer.

At the coronation the young Prince paid homage to the King, reciting the words: 'I, Edward, Prince of Wales, do become your liege man of life and limb and of earthly worship; and faith and truth I will bear unto you, to live and die against all manner of folks. So help me,

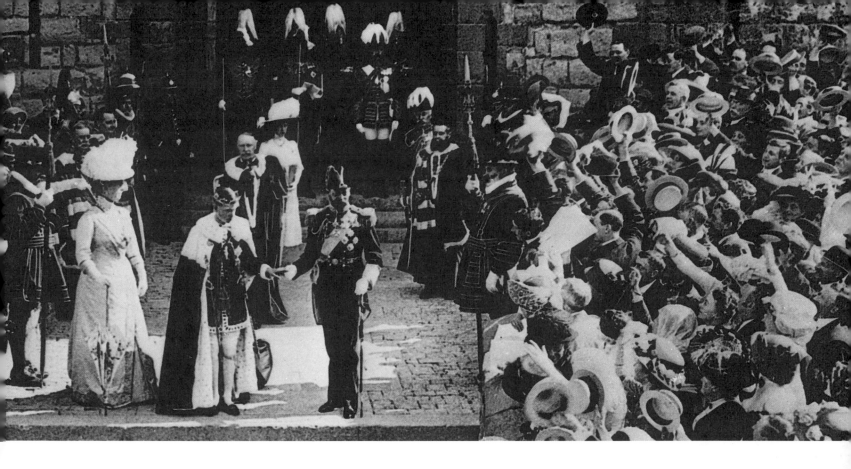

God.' He then kissed his father's cheek, and his father kissed his. That night the King recorded in his diary: 'I nearly broke down when dear David came to do homage to me, as it reminded me so much of when I did the same thing to beloved Papa, he did it so well.'

For Edward, however, the greatest ceremony came with his own investiture as Prince of Wales at Caernarvon Castle a few weeks later. The idea came, oddly, from that Welsh radical Lloyd George, attracted doubtless to the idea of a pageant in his native country. Lloyd George himself taught the Prince to speak a few sentences of Welsh: 'All Wales is a sea of song' and 'Thanks from the bottom of my heart to the old land of my fathers'. In his diary the King wrote: 'The dear boy did it remarkably well and looked so nice.' But in fact, as the Prince tells us in his memoirs, all did not go so smoothly.

The ceremony I had to go through with, the speech I had to make, and the Welsh I had to speak were, I thought, a sufficient ordeal for anyone. But when a tailor appeared to measure me for a fantastic costume designed for the occasion, consisting of white satin breeches and a mantle and surcoat of purple velvet edged with ermine, I decided things had gone too far. I had already submitted to the Garter dress and robe, for which there existed a condoning historical precedent; but what would my Navy friends say if they saw me in this preposterous rig? There was a family blow-up that night; but in the end my mother, as always, smoothed things over. 'You mustn't take a mere ceremony so seriously,' she said. 'Your friends will understand that as a Prince you are obliged to do certain things that may seem a little silly. It will be only for this once.'

And, reflecting on the ceremony, Prince Edward went even further:

When all this commotion was over, I made a painful discovery about myself. It was that, while I was prepared to fulfil my role in all this pomp and ritual, I recoiled from anything that tended to set me up as a person requiring homage. Even if my father was now beginning to remind me of the

Above The Prince of Wales tiger-shooting in Nepal.

The Prince of Wales embarked upon a series of triumphantly successful tours of the Empire and the United States after the war. His popularity was an immense asset to the monarch. *Below* the Prince of Wales as 'Chief Morning Star', the title given him by the Stony Creek Indians in Alberta during his Canadian tour, 1919.

obligations of my position, had he not been at pains to give me a strict and unaffected upbringing? And if my association with the village boys at Sandringham and the cadets of the Naval Colleges had done anything for me, it was to make me desperately anxious to be treated exactly like any other boy of my age.

Here indeed was a fatal misunderstanding of the role of monarchy. Homage was paid not to the person but to the office, to the institution. The heir to the throne was not 'like any other boy'. The failure to distinguish between the form of monarchy and the person of the king was to lead, eventually but inevitably, to all the squalid squalls which invaded his brief reign a quarter of a century in the future.

On leaving Dartmouth Edward had been obliged, unwillingly, to attend Magdalen College, Oxford, and also to spend periods of study in France and Germany to improve his knowledge of foreign languages. In these years he developed many of the characteristics that were to establish him as something of a 'Society Prince'. He welcomed his eighteenth birthday not because he was formally of age to succeed to the throne but because he could smoke in public. He enjoyed fast motoring, tennis and swimming in France, and made his first excursions to night clubs in Berlin. He also developed a taste for fashionable clothes, a taste which was not shared by his father. And by the summer of 1914 such entries were appearing in his diary as:

July 8th ...   To the Duke of Portland's house ... my dancing is improving. I got in at 4.
July 9th ...   I was up again at 6.00 & walked to Barracks ... on to Lady Salisbury's ball. ... I have now become fond of dancing & love going out ...
July 10th ...   I've had no more than 8 hrs. sleep in the last 72 hrs.!!

As these proclivities manifested themselves, so the King showed increasing displeasure with his son.

Prince Edward was just twenty years of age when the Great War began. Already it had been decided that he should leave Oxford and join the Grenadier Guards, and on the outbreak of hostilities the Prince desperately sought active service. As Frances Donaldson has said: 'It must be accepted that no emotion in his whole life was more sincere than his desire to serve and to suffer, if necessary to die, as every young man in the land might do except himself.' Frustration drips from the Prince's diary entries: 'I returned terribly depressed as of course the only topic was the war, & I haven't the remotest chance of getting out with the expeditionary force. . . . Oh!! that I had a job.' And when he thought he was to see active service, he wrote: 'I get away from this awful palace where I have had the worst weeks of my life!!' The Prince even sought an interview with Lord Kitchener: 'What does it matter if I am killed? I have four brothers.' Lord Kitchener replied candidly that the Prince's death was not the problem, but that his capture would prove embarrassing.

Although never involved in the active service he desired, the Prince was given staff appointments in France. Characteristically, he found it difficult to wear war decorations he had been awarded by virtue of his status while his comrades fought and died without recognition in the trenches. The sentiment is understandable, but again the Prince was seeing things as a person, an individual, rather than as representative of a historic institution. Yet despite his enforced withdrawal from action, he tirelessly squeezed the utmost from the opportunities he had. He was a frequent visitor to regiments at the Front and on several occasions put himself at personal risk. It was said, 'A bad shelling will always produce the Prince of Wales.' And his obvious courage and enthusiasm in this period earned for him the immense popularity with the British people that remained as long as he was Prince of Wales. Lord Esher wrote once to the Prince:

But in future, which may be full of unforeseen difficulties in the years far ahead, your gallantry and determination to live the life of a soldier and run the risks will never be forgotten. If it ever is, then our people will have lost all their noble traditions of regard for what is best in their princes and in the youth of our country.

Lord Esher, a trusted counsellor of the King, was an acute observer. On a visit to the Queen during the war, he 'tried to make her see that after the war thrones might be at a discount, and that the Prince of Wales's popularity might be a great asset'. Lloyd George, another acute observer, felt the same. Once victory was secured, the Prime Minister persuaded the King and Queen to send the Prince of Wales on goodwill tours of the Dominions. So in 1919 he visited Newfoundland, Canada and the United States, and the following year toured Australia and New Zealand, stopping at Honolulu, Fiji and the West Indies. And at the end of 1921 he set off once more, this time to India. Without doubt, the tours to America and to the Antipodes were a resounding success. The Prince's personality and boyishness gained an enthusiastic response from the cheering crowds

ABOVE The rakish 'Prince Charming' image. The Prince of Wales during his Canadian tour. His liveliness and sincerity captivated people wherever he went.

BELOW The Prince of Wales with Winston Churchill, Secretary of State for War, in 1919.

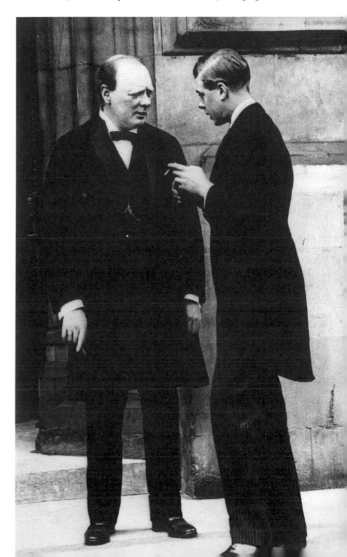

Edward at the races. He was, like his grandfather Edward VII, leader of a glittering social set.

which greeted him throughout the United States, Canada, Australia and New Zealand. The Indian tour was more difficult because of the mounting nationalist agitation there. Nonetheless, the Prince, though sometimes offending Indian sensibilities by his disregard for protocol, made a great success of the visit.

The King ought to have been proud of his son. The Prince's natural charm made him a perfect representative of the Crown. His earlier diffidence was giving way to greater self-assurance on public occasions, and his speeches, for which he sought help from the greatest of orators, Winston Churchill, were delivered with growing force and confidence.

Yet if the Prince's public life was beyond reproach, his private life was not; and the private life could not be withheld easily from the public. The King's attitude was well summed up in a letter he wrote to Albert, Duke of York, when he was married in 1923: 'You have always been so sensible & easy to work with & you have always been ready to listen to any advice & to agree with my opinions about people & things that I feel we have always got on very well together. Very different to dear David.'

There soon came jokes about the Prince falling in love only with married women, though in reality he fell deeply for only two. Mrs Dudley Ward he had met and fallen for early in 1918, and he remained devoted to her until 1934, when she was abruptly displaced by Mrs Simpson. If there are times when the Prince of Wales may have seemed casual or even superficial, there can be no doubting his capacity for complete, absolute adoration of the two women with whom he fell violently in love.

Freda Dudley Ward had first met the Prince through chance while sheltering from an air attack in a house in Belgrave Square. A party was in progress, and soon Mrs Ward found herself dancing with the Prince of Wales. He escorted her home that night. (By coincidence, the hostess was the sister of Ernest Simpson. Her future sister-in-law was to play an even more momentous part in the life of the Prince of Wales.) Mrs Dudley Ward soon became the dominating influence in the Prince's life. He telephoned her nearly every day and, whenever in London, would call on her, often staying far into the evening. There was little attempt to conceal the relationship. The couple were often to be seen dancing together at the fashionable Embassy Club, and society hostesses were soon aware that the presence of the Prince could be obtained only by the presence also of Mrs Dudley Ward.

Freda Dudley Ward had enormous charm. She was small, pretty and spoke in a voice described as 'oddly attractive'. The Prince thought, even at this early stage, of a marriage which might well necessitate his younger brother's replacing him as heir. But the depth of the Prince's feelings was never fully reciprocated by his mistress.

Prince Edward had other fleeting passions, and a firmer relationship with Lady Furness, who was both married and American. But his attachment to Mrs Dudley Ward remained firm until prised apart by his love for Mrs Wallis Simpson.

The elemental facts about Mrs Simpson were that she was an

American, a commoner and a married woman already once divorced. On one or other of these rocks the ship of monarchy might not have foundered. In the presence of all, the wreck was inevitable.

Wallis Warfield was born in Baltimore on 19 June 1896. She was therefore almost exactly two years younger than Prince Edward. Her family background, both on her mother's side and on her father's, was distinguished, and also, though she was not brought up in luxury, she did attend a select school in Baltimore, progress to a smart finishing school and 'come out' at a fashionable ball. She grew into an attractive girl, conscious of clothes and with a taste for parties and for the company of boys. She was not pretty; indeed her features were rather sharp, almost predatory. Her eyes were her great attraction, large and lustrous, and she had the uninhibited loquacity so characteristic of American girls. Her first marriage in 1916 was both unambitious and unsuccessful. Her husband, a naval air officer, called Earl Winfield Spencer Junior, was an alcoholic. He grew jealous of his wife's open flirtations at parties, while she in turn grew bored with her husband. They decided to separate, he to the Far East while she stayed in Washington. A brief and disastrous attempt at reconciliation followed in 1924, and eventually she obtained a divorce. In 1928 came her second marriage to Ernest Simpson, an American businessman. Simpson had been transferred to the London office of his father's shipping firm, and so the couple settled down to married life in a strange country.

Wallis enjoyed society, and she enjoyed entertaining. She gave elegant dinner parties at their luxurious flat in Bryanston Square and also regular cocktail parties, which were then in vogue. Gradually her circle widened, helped by contacts from her sister-in-law, that same lady under whose roof Prince Edward had first met Mrs Dudley Ward. Ironically, though, it was Lady Furness who first introduced Mrs Simpson to the Prince of Wales sometime in the autumn of 1930. No immediate attachment seems to have resulted. Indeed, the pair met on only a few occasions during the succeeding year.

Suddenly the Simpsons received a weekend invitation to Fort Belvedere, the house near Windsor Great Park which George V had given to his son. The guests were shown to their room, and they came down to the drawing-room to find the Prince sitting on a sofa doing needlepoint. 'This is to be a covering for a backgammon table,' he said. 'Sir,' Wallis replied, 'I am fascinated and impressed. But where, if I may ask, and how did you ever acquire this accomplishment?' The Prince replied: 'From my mother, when I was growing up. At Sandringham my brothers and sister and I used to sit around her at tea-time. While she talked to us she was either crocheting or doing some kind of embroidery; and because we were all interested she taught us *gros point*. I'm the only one of the four brothers who has kept it up. I find it relaxing and more useful than detective stories.' After dinner there were cards, and the Prince suggested they might try their hand at a complicated jigsaw puzzle. Later the gramophone was put on, and there was dancing. The Prince's first partner was Thelma Furness, and the tune was 'Tea For Two'.

The Prince of Wales had a most individual and carefully considered taste in dress. He worried about his clothes nearly as much as Edward VII had.

85

Wallis Simpson, the woman who held such an extraordinary and enigmatic fascination for Edward that he renounced a crown and a kingdom for her.

This was to be the first of many visits of the Simpsons to Fort Belvedere, and before long the Prince was in the habit of calling on Mrs Simpson at her London flat. By the beginning of 1934 society gossip was beginning to link their names. In May of that year Mrs Dudley Ward noticed that the usual telephone calls from the Prince had stopped. She called St James's Palace, and the telephonist recognized her voice. 'I have something so terrible to tell you that I don't know how to say it – I have orders not to put you through.' The new favourite was installed.

Discretion was no part of the royal romance, and within weeks the scandal was an open secret. The couple appeared frequently together, she loving to display the costly jewels the Prince had bestowed on her: 'bejewelled, eye-brow plucked, virtuous and wise', as Harold Nicolson remembered her. Lady Diana Cooper said that she 'dripped in new jewels and clothes', and some claimed that the Prince had given Wallis £50,000 worth of jewels at Christmas and £60,000 worth the following week to celebrate the New Year. Openly Mrs Simpson and the Prince went on summer cruises together. Mr Simpson now slipped into the background. A devoted royalist, he could not bring himself to remonstrate with the Prince.

In the autumn of 1934 Mrs Simpson was presented to the King and Queen for the only time, shortly before the Duke of Kent's wedding. Prince Edward had always had a close relationship with his younger brother, and this wedding marked the end of what was, we are told, outside love affairs. The King and Queen certainly knew of the Prince of Wales's infatuation for Mrs Simpson, and it is indeed a remarkable fact that father and son never spoke of the matter together. With uncanny accuracy the King predicted to Stanley Baldwin: 'After I am dead the boy will ruin himself in twelve months.' Shortly before his death, the King is said to have exclaimed: 'I pray to God that my eldest son will never marry and have children, and that nothing will come between Bertie and Lilibet and the throne.'

The new King's brief reign is inevitably coloured by the dramatic events of his abdication. Even the day-to-day details of the reign showed the King's preoccupation with Mrs Simpson. There was widespread criticism of his unpunctuality, arrogance and conceit, for as always he seems to have found it difficult to distinguish between the honour accorded him as king and as individual. He showed curious disregard for tradition and for the feelings of others. Within minutes of his father's death he had ordered all the clocks put back half an hour to the correct time, for since the days of Edward VII Sandringham time had always run in advance of Greenwich time. Again, he surrounded himself with those who were Mrs Simpson's friends and cut himself off from many lifelong friends and devoted servants who did not fall into this category. To be sure, as far as the public were aware, nothing was wrong. The new King was the same charming and popular man they had known as the Prince of Wales. And his appearances in industrial centres and visits to the unemployed in the mining towns and the depressed areas brought him enormous popularity.

King Edward VIII. He could have been the most popular king Britain had ever known. It had been generally hoped that after his father died Edward would bring fresh blood and a modern approach to the monarchy.

While the royal romance dominated the thoughts of the King and of many of the nation's leaders, cotton mills, docks and mines lay idle, and the heads of over a million families had no work. In Europe Hitler's Germany was set on the path that was to lead eventually to war, while Fascist Italy was swallowing her Ethiopian prey in Africa. 1936 saw, too, the outbreak of the Spanish Civil War, while in Asia China and Japan moved towards open conflict. Yet in Britain all events in the year 1936 seemed dwarfed by the momentous crisis which exploded at the end of that year.

The King exercising on board the yacht *Nahlin*. Edward was fanatical about exercise.

By the time of his accession the King had resolved to marry Mrs Simpson. This, perhaps, lay behind his uncontrollable grief at the death of his father. Until now the Prince's obsession could be a guilty, if open, secret. The King's obsession could not.

That summer the couple embarked on an ill-considered cruise to the Balkans. In Britain the newspapers, by mutual agreement, printed no details of the liaison. Photographs of the King, dressed only in shorts, standing side by side with Mrs Simpson, remained unpublished. But American papers had no such scruples, and slowly copies began to filter into England. Indeed, the affair became common knowledge to all except the mass of the British people. Critical letters began to arrive at Buckingham Palace and to reach the Archbishop of Canterbury, the Prime Minister, Queen Mary and other prominent figures.

Mrs Simpson, for her part, was as anxious to marry as the King, and accordingly she filed a divorce petition against her husband. The case was to be heard in Ipswich on 27 October. The King, anxious to avoid a blaze of publicity and the linking of his name with the divorce proceedings, sought and obtained help from Lord Beaverbrook and his Press colleagues. Thus the Press in Britain still remained silent, though abroad there was no such reticence.

As soon as he heard of the divorce petition, the Prime Minister, Stanley Baldwin, immediately sought an interview with the King. On 20 October Baldwin visited the King at Fort Belvedere and guardedly warned him of the difficulties his attachment to Mrs Simpson might cause. His object was to suggest that the divorce petition might be abandoned. The word 'marriage' was not mentioned. In the background stood Lang, Archbishop of Canterbury, fearful of being asked to crown a king who was wedded to a twice-divorced woman in defiance of the Church's teaching, fearful also of crowning Mrs Simpson queen of England.

Matters now moved speedily to a climax. On Friday 13 November, as the King returned to Fort Belvedere after a gruelling and sodden visit to the Fleet at Southampton, he found a document waiting marked 'Urgent and Confidential'. The message was from Alexander Hardinge, his Principal Private Secretary. It brought the unwelcome news that, 'The silence of the British Press on the subject of Your Majesty's friendship with Mrs Simpson is *not* going to be maintained. It is probably only a matter of days before the outburst begins.' Even worse, the affair, if pressed to a conclusion, might bring the resignation of the government, in which case no alternative government could be formed, 'in view of the feeling prevalent among members of the House of Commons of all parties'. And finally, worst of all, came the advice to send Mrs Simpson abroad *'without further delay'*.

The King now turned to his close friend Walter Monckton, in whom he had already confided his intention to marry Mrs Simpson. Monckton, a brilliant barrister, agreed to act as adviser and intermediary in the King's dealings with Baldwin. The meeting with Monckton took place on the Sunday following the receipt of

Hardinge's message, and Edward told Monckton of his determination to send for Baldwin and tell him that if the government could not reconcile itself to his marriage, he was indeed prepared to abdicate. The King also wired to Lord Beaverbrook, then on a voyage to America, urging him to return at once. Lord Beaverbrook obliged and on arrival at New York promptly returned on the same ship.

The following day, 16 November, the King summoned Baldwin to Buckingham Palace. This time there was no shirking the issue. The Prime Minister informed the King that he did not consider that his

The picture the British public never saw: King Edward and Mrs Simpson sightseeing at Trogir during their Adriatic cruise in the *Nahlin* during the summer of 1936.

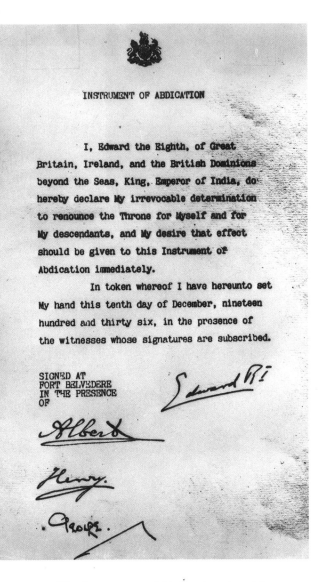

INSTRUMENT OF ABDICATION

I, Edward the Eighth, of Great Britain, Ireland, and the British Dominions beyond the Seas, King, Emperor of India, do hereby declare My irrevocable determination to renounce the Throne for Myself and for My descendants, and My desire that effect should be given to this Instrument of Abdication immediately.

In token whereof I have hereunto set My hand this tenth day of December, nineteen hundred and thirty six, in the presence of the witnesses whose signatures are subscribed.

SIGNED AT
FORT BELVEDERE
IN THE PRESENCE
OF

The Instrument of Abdication signed by Edward and his three brothers, the Dukes of York, Gloucester and Kent.

Opposite The Duke and Duchess of Windsor on their wedding day, 3 June 1937, at the Chateau de Condé, France. A photograph by Cecil Beaton.

marriage with Mrs Simpson 'would receive the approbation of the country'. The King told Baldwin: 'I want you to be the first to know that I have made up my mind and nothing will alter it – I have looked at it from all sides – and I mean to abdicate to marry Mrs Simpson.' Baldwin responded: 'Sir, this is a very grave decision and I am deeply grieved.' Nothing could shake the resolve of the King, and Baldwin recorded later that at the interview, 'The King's face wore at times such a look of beauty as might have lighted the face of a young knight who had caught a glimpse of the Holy Grail.'

That night, Edward broke the painful news to his mother, Queen Mary. The Queen was shocked, angry and humiliated and refused Edward's request that she should receive Wallis Simpson. The following day the King informed his brothers. Albert, the heir presumptive, was so stunned that he could not utter a single word.

Edward still had slight hopes that the situation might be saved. Monckton, Duff Cooper, Beaverbrook, Winston Churchill and others of the King's supporters tried in various ways to find a solution. There was some talk of a morganatic marriage, whereby the children of the marriage would have no right of succession. There was talk, too, of postponing the wedding until after the coronation in May. But the Dominions were implacably opposed to the first solution, as indeed were many in the Cabinet and also Clement Attlee, leader of the Labour Party, while the King would not consider the second alternative.

On 2 December the Press broke its long silence. The northern newspapers seized the opportunity to comment on remarks by the Bishop of Bradford which were interpreted as referring to the King's affair with Mrs Simpson. The following day the national papers, critical and sorrowful, splashed the story. Mrs Simpson, to avoid the now inevitable glare of publicity, left promptly for France. Edward remained to face the last agonizing nine days of his reign.

For a few days longer, shut in the seclusion of Fort Belvedere, receiving daily telephone calls from Wallis Simpson in Cannes, hope still flickered. Churchill spoke gallantly of a 'King's Party', and the King himself thought of broadcasting his case to the people, a suggestion which the Cabinet would not countenance. But the harsh fact was that the overwhelming majority of the public, and the Dominions, backed Stanley Baldwin. There was no broad basis of support for a struggle.

By Monday 7 December the King had determined finally that there was no alternative but to abdicate. Still a few desperate efforts were made. At this eleventh hour Wallis Simpson offered to withdraw from the proposed marriage, but to Edward this was unthinkable. Nothing now could apparently change the course of events.

On Thursday morning, 10 December, the Instrument of Abdication was signed, witnessed by the King's three brothers. That afternoon his message was read by the Speaker to the House of Commons. The following day Edward ceased to be King of England, and that evening, as 'His Royal Highness Prince Edward', he broadcast a farewell message to the British people:

The Duke and Duchess of Windsor in 1966.

At long last I am able to say a few words of my own. I have never wanted to withhold anything, but until now it has been not constitutionally possible for me to speak. A few hours ago I discharged my last duty as King and Emperor, and now that I have been succeeded by my brother, the Duke of York, my first words must be to declare my allegiance to him. This I do with all my heart. You all know the reasons which have impelled me to renounce the throne. But I want you to understand that in making up my mind I did not forget the country or the Empire which as Prince of Wales, and lately as King, I have for twenty-five years tried to serve. But you must believe me when I tell you that I have found it impossible to carry the heavy burden of responsibility and to discharge my duties as King as I would wish to do without the help and support of the woman I love.

And Edward concluded:

I now quit altogether public affairs and I lay down my burden. It may be some time before I return to my native land, but I shall always follow the fortunes of the British race and Empire with profound interest, and if at any time in the future I can be found of service to His Majesty in a private station, I shall not fail. And now we all have a new King. I wish him and you, his people, happiness and prosperity with all my heart. God bless you all. God save the King.

So the ex-King left for France and his beloved Wallis. In April the decree nisi, granted the year previously at Ipswich, became absolute. The Duke of Windsor – for this was the title his brother had bestowed upon him – married Wallis in June, the month after his brother had been crowned King of England. For the remainder of their lives the devoted couple lived a strange, exiled existence, spent mainly in Paris and New York. There was much bitterness: bitterness because the Duchess, though married to a royal Duke, was not permitted the title 'Her Royal Highness'; bitterness because of the long, degrading exile from Britain; bitterness because, despite frantic appeals for a wartime post, reminiscent of the young Prince's agitation in the First World War, nothing better could be found than the Governorship of a West Indian island. Edward returned to his native land only a few times after the war. He came for sorrowful occasions such as the funeral of his brother King George VI, and for the unveiling by Queen Elizabeth in 1967 of a plaque in memory of his mother Queen Mary. But from the coronation celebrations of 1953 he was conspicuously absent.

Early in 1972 it became known that the Duke was desperately ill, dying from cancer of the throat. The Queen, on an official visit to France, saw her uncle at his bedside. She spoke also to the Duchess: the presence of death had at last brought reconciliation.

A few days after the Queen's visit, on 28 May, the Duke died, nearly seventy-eight years of age. Only then did the British people seem ready to forget and forgive. In death he was treated with honour and respect by his family and nation, his body flown home from Paris to lie in state for two days in St George's Chapel at Windsor. Queues formed more than a mile in length, and nearly sixty thousand people filed past the body. Many recalled once more his charm, his youth and his promise, his sympathy for the unemployed and for the suffering soldiers – above all, perhaps, his obsession for a woman that reached beyond love to a point almost of madness. The Duchess at long last was a guest at Buckingham Palace, and the ceremony in St George's Chapel was conducted in the presence of the Royal Family. The body of the Duke was finally laid to rest near his brother's at Frogmore.

The Duke and Duchess of Windsor with the Queen at Marlborough House in 1967 for the unveiling of a plaque commemorating the centenary of Queen Mary's birth. It was their first public appearance in the company of the Queen.

CHAPTER FOUR

George VI

'This is absolutely terrible. I never wanted this to happen; I'm quite unprepared for it. David has been trained for this all his life. I've never even seen a State Paper. I'm only a naval officer, it's the only thing I know about.' This was George VI's appalled reaction to his elevation as he watched his brother preparing to leave the country.

The new King was certainly unprepared mentally – he was happier than he had ever been, leading the relatively obscure, contented family life into which he had settled since his marriage, and he dreaded the upheaval. He was even more unprepared from the practical point of view. His elder brother had experienced great difficulty in extracting any sort of information on affairs of state from George V, and *he* had expected to be the next king: Prince Albert, a mere younger son, had been positively dissuaded when he had attempted to familiarize himself with the workings of the government. Yet despite his enormous self-doubts, as George VI he won the sincere affection and admiration of his people, largely through his steadfast example during the Second World War which overshadowed his reign. He came to epitomize the calm resolution of the British people and the determination of Britain and her Commonwealth allies to hold out against German military might, however overwhelming the odds. In particular he epitomized the courage of London during the Blitz, when events seemed to have reached their lowest ebb and when Britain, still without the support of the United States, appeared unlikely to survive for very long.

At the time the mere presence of George VI and his wife, Queen Elizabeth, became an invaluable boost to morale. By his clear desire to stay and share every experience totally, from being bombed to eating whale meat, he earned a place in the history books as a good man and a successful monarch. It was a very different reputation from the one which might have been expected of the diffident, rather unimpressive man who came to the throne in such an unlikely and unexpected way.

Prince Albert was the second son of the Duke and Duchess of York. He was born on 14 December 1895 and called 'Albert' after his great-grandfather, for this date was the anniversary of the Prince Consort's death thirty-four years previously and it was felt necessary to give him the name rather as a way of apologizing to Queen Victoria for the ill-chosen day of his birth. His childhood, although punctuated with

Opposite King George VI in the uniform of rear-admiral.

A photograph of Prince Albert as a young child with his mother Princess Mary on one of the rare occasions when she showed maternal feelings towards her younger son.

happy moments, particularly the time spent with his doting and easy-going grandparents Edward VII and Queen Alexandra, was not overall a happy experience. He was naturally shy and introverted and his childhood experiences did nothing to reverse these traits. Albert, like Edward, suffered from lack of parental warmth, and especially from the gruff discipline of George V. Edward always had a natural resilience which enabled him to overcome this, although we know from his writing in later life that he felt it keenly. He also had the advantage of knowing that he was his father's heir, and therefore had an importance all his own. Albert had none of these advantages and he was permanently affected by his upbringing. His mother, Queen Mary was happy to leave her five children to the care of nannies, as was the custom in aristocratic families of the time. Unfortunately she showed little interest in the way in which her nursery was run, and for two years the boys were in the care of that nanny who doted on the elder brother. Prince Albert she ignored almost totally; it has even been suggested that his constant ill health in later life was a result of her early neglect. Although she was eventually dismissed and replaced with a much more motherly woman, great damage had been done in those crucial early years. The outward sign of Prince Albert's inner conflicts was a very noticeable stammer which became worse at times of stress, and therefore was very apparent when he had to make any sort of public appearance. He was naturally left-handed but was forced to use his right hand, which put even more strain on him. When, at the age of thirteen, he took the entrance examination for Osborne, the junior naval college, he was considered to be the most nervous candidate the interviewers had ever seen.

For such a socially inept child Osborne was a further traumatic experience. He had been used to sharing a classroom with just one brother and at Osborne he was one of seventy cadets in the same year. With time he settled in and became well-liked, with friends of his own and quite a reputation as a sportsman, but his academic record was abysmal, and after two years he came last in the entrance examination for Dartmouth. His tutor was forced to admit: 'I am afraid there is no disguising the fact that Prince Albert has gone a mucker....'

At Dartmouth his academic performance was no better, though he tried extremely hard, but his athletic prowess increased and he established his ability to get on well with those around him. His closest friend was Dr Louis Greig, a surgeon-lieutenant sixteen years his senior, whom he had met at Osborne when Greig treated him for a bad cold. Louis Greig had a unique capacity for bringing out the best in Prince Albert, and he remained a close friend for years. It was he who encouraged the Prince to play tennis with his left hand. Together they won the RAF doubles championship in 1920 and later competed at Wimbledon.

In January 1913 Prince Albert finished his training with a tour of duty on the cruiser *Cumberland*; his friend Louis Greig was posted to the same ship as part of the medical team. The *Cumberland* went to Tenerife, the West Indies and Canada. It is a gauge of how much the role of the monarchy has changed since those days that in 1913 Prince Albert wrote home indignantly of the Americans, 'who had no manners at all and tried to take photographs all the time'. In spite of this, he proved a success both as a sailor, despite a tendency to sea-sickness and, despite his diffidence, as a royal representative ashore.

In September he was appointed a midshipman on HMS *Collingwood* and was still on the *Collingwood* when war broke out in August 1914. His war service was frequently interrupted by gastric illness causing the Prince great distress for he was as anxious as his elder brother to undertake active service. These illnesses were also an embarrassment to the naval authorities, who thought his frequent spells in hospital and of shore duty might be misinterpreted as favouritism. This was certainly not the case. George V was himself a sailor by training and inclination and understood his son's desire to do his duty. When, in 1915, Prince Albert consented to go onto the hospital ship only on condition he was allowed back on the *Collingwood* if there was any action, the King wrote to the surgeons who had expressed their doubts about his fitness for battle: 'The King would prefer to run the risk of Prince Albert's health suffering than that he should endure the bitter and lasting disappointment of not being in his ship in the battle line.'

In 1916, after another period of convalescence ashore, the Prince returned to his ship in time to take part in the battle of Jutland against the German High Seas Fleet. The *Collingwood* was in the thick of the fighting, for the cruiser squadron was under heavy attack from the German battleships. Afterwards Prince Albert wrote to his elder brother, who was then with the Army in France: 'When I was on top of the turret, I never felt any fear of shells or anything else. It seems curious but all sense of danger and everything else goes except the one longing of dealing death in every possible way to the enemy.'

A few weeks later the gastric trouble recurred and was eventually diagnosed as a duodenal ulcer. A period of rest appeared to cure it, although Prince Albert fretted at yet another spell ashore. In May 1917 he joined the battleship *Malaya*, again with Dr Louis Greig in attendance. However, it soon became apparent that an operation would be the only lasting cure for the ulcer, and this was performed at the end of 1917. It meant an end to his naval career, for the ulcer had gone undetected too long and he no longer had the stamina for active service. He therefore transferred to the RNAS and went to Cranwell, then a rather primitive training college for officers of the newest branch of the armed forces, the Flying Corps. George V had recently given the Flying Corps the title 'Royal', and by sending Prince Albert to Cranwell he was able to emphasize its importance yet again.

The Prince was in charge of training the boys' squadron and proved himself a stern disciplinarian. He himself did not learn to fly until the war had ended. In 1919 he took flying lessons, together with his friend Louis Greig, and became the first member of the Royal Family to qualify as a pilot. Yet he was again thwarted by ill health, for the doctors forbade him to fly solo, which meant that to stay in the Air Force, as in the Navy, he would have to accept a desk job.

Above Prince Albert, known to the family as Bertie, in the Royal Navy in 1914. Despite increasingly bad health, he served as a sub-lieutenant during the battle of Jutland, 1916.

Below The Duke of York playing tennis at Wimbledon in 1926. He and his partner, Dr Louis Greig, where beaten in the first round.

But after 'the War to end all Wars' careers in the Navy and the Air Force were no longer real propositions for the Princes. During the post-war period Prince Albert sought for something worthwhile to occupy his time. Although he often represented his father on public occasions, he still suffered from the nervous stammer which made such occasions a trial to him. Moreover, his father consistently denied him any access to state papers so he had no insight into the workings of government and the monarchy to compensate for the purely ceremonial function he was allowed to fulfil.

Just as he had done when Bertie was a boy, the King continued to make decisions about what his children should do. He decided that Albert, and his younger brother Prince Henry, should spend some time at Cambridge. They were attached to Trinity College but did not live in college itself like the majority of undergraduates: instead, recalling Edward VII's youthful seclusion, they were installed in a private house with Louis Greig as equerry. The King had insisted on this because he said it would give them a greater measure of freedom, but it meant that the Princes were physically cut off from much day-to-day undergraduate life, in addition to their inevitable isolation because of who they were. The King had also insisted that only one year's study was necessary, and since that one year was interrupted by attending state and public functions, it offered only a taste of what Cambridge life could be. Nevertheless, with Louis Greig's help Prince

Albert made what he could of the year. 'My principal contribution was to put steel into him,' Greig later said of this period. The Prince was inclined to give up too easily when faced with defeat in something competitive like golf or tennis. Greig taught him to cope with losing and to strive for success.

In June 1920, aged twenty-four, he came down from Cambridge and was created Duke of York by his father in the Birthday Honours. In 1922 he fell in love with Lady Elizabeth Bowes-Lyon, the youngest daughter of the fourteenth Earl of Strathmore and Kinghorne. They had first met as adults in 1920, and she had been a bridesmaid at the wedding of his sister Princess Mary to the sixth Earl of Harewood in 1922. Elizabeth Bowes-Lyon was a pretty and popular girl with great charm, and she was not short of admirers. She even managed to work her charm on George V, who told his son, 'You'll be a lucky fellow if she accepts you.'

Throughout 1922 the Duke of York was frequently a visitor in the Bowes-Lyon household, either at their Mayfair home, their country house at Walden Bury or their Scottish home, Glamis Castle. His

Below The wedding day. The bridal couple with their parents the Earl and Countess of Strathmore and King George V and Queen Mary.

Queen Elizabeth with the Princesses Elizabeth and Margaret in the grounds of Windsor Castle.

devotion was overwhelming, but it took him a long time to gather his courage for a proposal, believing as he did that a king's son should not place himself in the embarrassing position of possibly being refused. Eventually, early in 1923, he did propose and was accepted. The couple were married on 26 April of the same year at Westminster Abbey, before three thousand guests. The last time a royal prince had married in the Abbey had been in 1383 when Richard II married Anne of Bohemia, and the 1923 decision to hold such a public ceremony instead of the customary private wedding in one of the royal chapels showed an acceptance of the increasingly public nature of the monarchy and an awareness that no ideal opportunity to exploit royal pageantry and ceremony should be allowed to slip by. The Archbishop of York, who assisted at the ceremony, referred to the public nature of the wedding in his address to the young couple: 'The warm and generous heart of this people takes you today unto itself. Will you not in response take that heart, with all its joys and sorrows, unto your own?'

Albert and his family were popular with the public. There can be no doubt that the grace and charm which has remained so character-istic of the Queen Mother did a great deal to foster and cement public feelings. They continued to present a picture of married hap-piness for the rest of their lives together, and the public response to their wedding had shown how important this image was for the continuing success of the British monarchy, particularly at a time when European monarchs were being ousted from their thrones.

After the wedding George V wrote to the Duke of York:

You are indeed a lucky man to have such a charming and delightful wife as Elizabeth, and I am sure you will both be very happy together, and I trust you both will have many, many years of happiness before you, and that you will be as happy as Mama and I are after you have been married for thirty years, I can't wish you more. . . . I am quite certain that Elizabeth will be a splendid partner in your work and share with you and help you in all you have to do.

He could not know that the Duke of York's role was to change dramatically when his elder brother abdicated and brought him to the throne, but he was quite right in predicting that the new Duchess of York would prove a tower of strength to her husband at every moment of his life, especially during the traumatic period when he first became king.

One of the first and most important ways in which the new Duchess helped her husband was in overcoming his stammer. Her own happy childhood and close family life had given her a confidence which she was able to communicate to him, and it enabled her to create a similar ambience in their own home. When their two children were born, Princess Elizabeth in 1926 and Princess Margaret in 1930, they created their own miniature version of the close-knit Bowes-Lyon family. With a secure home and a family in whose affection and support he could feel confident, the time was ripe for the Duke of York to tackle his disabling stammer. It seems unlikely that any cure would have worked earlier, in the stifling atmosphere of his parents' home where he was frequently criticized and rebuffed, although he visited many specialists and constantly tried to beat the problem by

Windsor Castle. Its history goes back to the time of William the Conqueror and it is the only one of the royal homes to compare in tradition to Queen Elizabeth's ancestral home, Glamis Castle in Scotland, which featured in the stories of both Mary Queen of Scots and Bonny Prince Charlie.

will-power alone. It was fortuitous that in 1926 the Duke was introduced to an Australian speech-therapist, Lionel Logue. He had naturally rather despaired of any good coming from these endless visits to speech therapists, and it was his wife who persuaded him to make this one last attempt.

Logue was not a qualified medical practitioner, but he had a strong personality and an ability to bolster up people whose spirit had been worn down by the humiliation of a speech defect. Once he had inspired the patient to tackle the problem, the treatment was based on a series of breathing exercises which developed the lungs and gave an understanding of breathing rhythm. This treatment suited the Duke of York, particularly as Logue emphasized that it was the patient's own responsibility to put the treatment into practice, an attitude which appealed to the Duke's strong sense of personal discipline. 'There is only one person who can cure you, and that is yourself,' said Logue. 'I can tell you what to do, but only you can do it.' After only a month the Duke wrote to his father: 'I have been seeing Logue every day, and I have noticed a great improvement in my talking, and also in making speeches which I did this week. I am sure I am going to get quite all right in time, but twenty-four years of talking in the wrong way cannot be cured in a month. I wish I could have found him before, as now that I know the right way to breathe my fear of talking will vanish.'

The Duke's speech did improve, although his stammer was always liable to recur when he was tired or worried. Nevertheless, once the problem over making public speeches had virtually disappeared, he was still given very little opportunity for public service while his father was King. Already the First World War, by virtually clearing away the vestiges of a Europe run by inter-related dynasties, had made it abundantly clear just how little power the monarch really did have. Royal prestige was simply another tool of government, and a major way in which members of the Royal Family could serve their country was as emissaries abroad.

The Prince of Wales himself was given little introduction to the monarch's working life by his father, despite the fact that he was heir apparent, yet at least he was kept hard at work on overseas visits. The Duke of York did not even have that consolation. Soon after the war he had represented Britain at two family events in the Balkans where the government was anxious to make the British presence felt, and in 1924 he had visited Northern Ireland when the government wanted to reassure the Stormont Parliament that it was not being neglected in favour of Southern Ireland. In 1925 he paid a short visit to the East African colonies. These were all relatively minor excursions. In 1926 he and the Duchess undertook the only tour of any importance that he was called upon to make. This was a tour of Australia and New Zealand to open the new Parliament building in Canberra. It was an important tour because the Dominions, including Australia and New Zealand, were moving away from Britain's influence, as Britain refused to give them the trade concessions they wanted. The symbolic importance of the monarchy

Opposite Complementary portraits of the Duchess and Duke of York, 1931, by Philip de Laszlo.

Right The Duke and Duchess of York visit the Isle of Skye in 1933.

as a focus for Commonwealth and Imperial unity was therefore more important than ever. The antipodean tour was an undoubted success in both countries. The Duchess, as always, inspired warm affection, while the Duke was appreciated for his unmistakeable sincerity. With his stammer brought under control and his wife by his side, the Duke was a confident and attractive royal ambassador, even evoking the sort of ardent response that his brother David did on his many tours.

Unhappily, on the royal couple's return from what had been an undoubted triumph, George V failed to show any appreciation of what everyone agreed had been a job well done. In spite of his eagerness to serve, the Duke of York was not called upon to make any further tours.

Denied both a spectacular role abroad and any insight into the work of the monarchy at home, the Duke attempted to find a satisfactory and constructive way to fill his time. The country was suffering from the effects of the Depression, and the Duke keenly felt the need to familiarize himself with the workings of finance and industry and with the actual conditions of workers. He visited factories and mines, anxious to understand as much as possible about a way of life which, with his background, he could never fully comprehend. Nevertheless his efforts were generally appreciated, for they showed that the monarchy, in spite of its privilege and wealth, had not totally forgotten the realities of life for so many millions of the people, and ever since it has been taken for granted that members of the Royal Family will visit and encourage industry.

The Duke of York became the first president of the Industrial Welfare Society, a well-meaning organization which, in spite of criticisms that it was paternalistic, fulfilled a useful function during the period of heavy unemployment that resulted from the Depression and the Slump. It sought to make employers aware of their responsibilities to their employees and encouraged the creation of pension funds and of facilities for health and welfare schemes at a time when there was no Welfare State to undertake the majority of these responsibilities. It was by no means a radical society – the Duke of York was certainly a very conservative man, but his involvement reflected his real concern to put the prestige of the monarchy to practical use.

Another project with which he was intimately associated, more so even than with the IWS since it was largely his own idea, was the establishment of annual boys' camps. The aim of these camps was to bring together boys from all types of background in an environment in which they could forget their social and economic differences and the antagonisms such differences provoked, by concentrating on activities which they had in common. In effect the camps provided sporting holidays for lads aged between seventeen and nineteen from public schools and from industry.

The Duke took a keen personal interest in the camps, and it was largely because of this royal patronage that firms could be persuaded to sponsor their young employees. Several wealthy industrialists, as well as giving paid leave to employees, also donated sums of money to fund the camps. The Duke of York often took part himself, and for the final camp, in 1939, he took a group of two hundred to the holiday home of his childhood, Abergeldie Castle. Like the IWS, the camps were not part of a radical concept. They sought to foster co-operation rather than confrontation as a means of solving the country's very obvious social difficulties. They typified both the Duke's good intentions and also his lack of really imaginative responses to the problems of the time.

However, these projects gave the Duke a sense of purpose and fulfilment which, together with his happy home life, made this an extremely contented period. He and his family lived the ideal life still possible for a wealthy aristocratic family before the war, even a family with a social conscience. The Duke enjoyed shooting and was a good shot. He enjoyed too all the other traditional country pastimes, including riding and fishing. At Royal Lodge, Windsor, to which the family moved after the Slump, he became involved in laying out the gardens and soon became an expert landscape gardener. Denied the chance to take a real part in the monarchy or the government, he withdrew more and more into the happiness of his private life until the shock of the abdication jolted him back into public life with a vengeance.

Through the trauma of the abdication period the Duke acted with great dignity, despite Edward's refusal to discuss these crucial matters with his brother. On acceding to the throne he chose the name 'George' to emphasize the continuity of the monarchy despite the

Above King George and Queen Elizabeth in the gold state coach after the opening of Parliament in 1938.

Opposite George VI and Queen Elizabeth in their coronation robes. The great day was marked by solemn pageantry. The King had to restore prestige to the monarchy after the abdication.

Overleaf The royal luncheon at the Guildhall to celebrate the coronation of King George VI and Queen Elizabeth, by Frank Salisbury.

abdication. The new King was crowned on 12 May 1937, the day formerly arranged for the coronation of Edward VIII. Prime Minister Baldwin, who had done his best to modify the effects of the abdication, retired in the same month. However, knowing the new King's desperate lack of political knowledge and experience, he worked hard to teach George VI as much as possible before he left, and after his retirement Baldwin continued to be as helpful as he could; he introduced the King to many influential people, particularly members of the Labour Party whom he could not expect to meet during the normal course of events.

George V had realized that a king must always support his Prime Minister, and it was one political lesson George VI had learned from his father. When Neville Chamberlain came to office after Baldwin, he naturally gave him the same support. The King had an instinctive dislike of Germany's aggressive policies in Europe and was torn between a feeling that they must be stopped and the desire, in common with most of the British people, to avoid war. Like the rest of the country, he welcomed the reprieve that Chamberlain's Munich Agreement of September 1938 seemed to bring. Chamberlain's policy of Appeasement has been overwhelmingly condemned in retrospect, yet at the time it seemed the most sensible course. The Labour Opposition, which opposed any sort of re-armament, supported it. The mass of the British people, who rightly feared another devastating confrontation, like the First World War only twenty years previously, welcomed it. So it was not surprising that the King agreed with his Prime Minister, whose own party (apart from a few hard-liners like Winston Churchill and Anthony Eden) was in favour of it. On 2 October the King issued a message of thanksgiving in which he said: 'After the magnificent efforts of the Prime Minister in the cause of peace, it is my fervent hope that a new era of friendship and prosperity may be dawning among the peoples of the world.' At least after Munich there could be no doubt where the blame lay when war did break out, and this was some consolation to the King.

It came as a tremendous shock when the Germans occupied Czechoslovakia in March the following year, as this was the very event which the Munich meeting had been intended to prevent. Too late, as Churchill had predicted, the British government began hastily to prepare for the real possibility of war and to put together a series of alliances to oppose the Germans. At last the King could be of real use, and he could support the new policy secure in the knowledge that Britain had done everything possible in the search for peace. In May he and the Queen undertook an exhausting tour of Canada and the United States. His visit to Canada undoubtedly helped kindle support for the mother country. As Lord Tweedsmuir, the Governor General of Canada said: 'The visit was a demonstration of our unity of spirit.' Only the King could have evoked the sentimental awareness of Canada's historic tie with Britain. His visit to the United States was equally significant, especially since it was the first time a reigning British monarch had visited the country. Eleanor Roosevelt later wrote:

Flask Walk, Hampstead on Coronation Day, 1937, by Charles Ginner. The nation welcomed its new King with regret but also an element of relief.

My husband invited them to Washington largely because, believing that we all might soon be engaged in a life and death struggle, in which Great Britain would be our first line of defence, he hoped that the visit would create a bond of friendship between the people of the two countries. He knew that, though there is always in this country a certain amount of criticism and ill-feeling toward the British, in time of danger something deeper comes to the surface, and the British and we stand firmly together, with confidence in our common heritage and ideas. The visit of the King and Queen, he hoped would be a reminder of this deep bond. In many ways it proved even more successful than he had expected.

After the official talks and receptions in Washington, the Roosevelts invited the King and Queen to spend a few days at their country home, Hyde Park, on the Hudson River. This gave the two men a chance for more private talks, in which they established a real rapport which was cemented by their regular correspondence afterwards.

At that time there were good reasons for fearing that the United States would not readily come to Britain's aid. Since the First World War, the United States had retreated into a firmly isolationist position, confident that it had the resources to be totally self-sufficient and regarding the conflicts in Europe as irrelevant. This attitude was typified by the attitude of Joseph Kennedy, the United States Ambassador to Britain, who could find nothing good to say of Britain in his reports home. Roosevelt, however, was more flexible in his outlook and recognized the likelihood of the United States' eventually becoming involved in a European war. He implied as much to George VI, who meticulously noted down everything that was said and reported it back. The relative success of these talks and the favourable impression made on the people of the United States by the royal couple were valuable factors in re-establishing vital links with the United States. Until the United States entered the war, she made a contribution in terms of money and equipment and eventually agreed to the fuller lend-lease arrangements. There is no doubt that his friendship with the King encouraged the pro-British Roosevelt to force these vital measures through the basically anti-British Congress and Senate.

On 22 August 1939, only a few days after coming to an agreement with Soviet Russia, Germany invaded Poland, and so, in accordance with their obligations, Britain and France declared war. On Sunday 3 September the King broadcast to the nation:

For the second time in the lives of most of us we are at war. Over and over again we have tried to find a peaceful way out of the differences between ourselves and those who are now our enemies. But it has been in vain. We have been forced into a conflict. For we are called, with our allies, to meet the challenge of a principle which, if it were to prevail, would be fatal to any civilized order in the world.

He asked the people of the Empire and Commonwealth to stand firm with Britain, and the Commonwealth Prime Ministers made it clear that their support could be counted upon.

Left A Second World War poster appealing to Englishmen to defend their pleasant, peaceful country from devastation and invasion.

Above The little ships at Dunkirk during that legendary June in 1940 when 224,000 British and 111,000 French troops were rescued by fleets of small craft assisting the Navy and merchant seamen.

The King, as the focal point and symbol of the Commonwealth and Empire, now had a unique opportunity to boost morale and encourage unity. He chose to do it in the calm, quiet way which suited him best. He spoke frequently on the radio, and although he was no fiery orator, his obvious sincerity and love for his people inspired genuine affection and made everyone aware that the King represented a way of life which was worth fighting for.

In the summer of 1940 the Germans began their heavy bombing of British cities after the Battle of Britain had effectively prevented an immediate invasion. Because of the unwillingness of the government until the last few months of 1939 to face up to the reality of war, the cities were desperately unprepared – even Buckingham Palace did not have its own air-raid shelter – which underlined the fact that the Royal Family was facing exactly the same privations and dangers as the rest of the people. The King and Queen had chosen to stay in London despite the danger, thereby emphasizing the role of the monarchy as the symbol of the nation as a whole. In spite of the terrible devastation, the Blitz is remembered for the remarkable community spirit which flourished amid the chaos. This, and the spirit of resistance which went hand in hand with it, was greatly fostered by the presence of the King and Queen. They visited the bombed areas, offering sympathy and encouragement, making it clear that those who bore the brunt of the bombing were in fact fighting a vital battle in the defence of the country. To heighten this feeling still further, the King created two new awards, the George Cross and the George Medal, for civilian workers whose acts of bravery could not be rewarded with military medals. He directed that these should rank second only to the Victoria Cross. Twice Buckingham Palace itself was bombed, once when the King and Queen were watching from a window. Afterwards the Queen made the famous remark: 'I'm glad we've been bombed: it makes me feel I can look the East End in the face.'

By this time Britain was being led by a coalition government with Winston Churchill as Prime Minister. Despite a firm belief that it was his duty to support his Prime Minister, George VI had viewed the prospect of Churchill with some misgivings in view of Churchill's quixotic espousal of his brother's cause during the abdication crisis. However, members of all parties had made it clear that they would not serve in a coalition headed by Chamberlain, and the only other main contender for the position, Lord Halifax, had been a committed supporter of the policy of Appeasement. He also had an anachronistic patrician manner which made him unpopular with the Labour Party. So Churchill, who had been preaching the need for re-armament while Chamberlain pursued his policy of Appeasement, became the man to lead Britain through the war itself.

The initial distrust between the King and Churchill soon turned into friendship. The Prime Minister's regular weekly audiences with the King were replaced by Tuesday lunches, and by 1941 the King was able to write in the diary which he kept throughout the war, 'I could not have a better Prime Minister.' Indeed, Churchill, with his tenacity

After the Battle of Britain the Germans stepped up their bombing campaigns. *Above* St Paul's, the morning after the bombing, by W. A. Golding.

Right A German Messerschmidt which crashed in Windsor Great Park caused intense local excitement.

Above St Clement Dane's Church on fire after being bombed, 1941.

Left The King inspecting the devastation of Coventry Cathedral after the Germans bombed the city on the night of 14 November, 1940. Five hundred aircraft had dropped 543 tons of explosive on the city.

Churchill, Roosevelt and Stalin at the Yalta Conference, February 1945. It was the last peace-talk of the 'Big Three'. Stalin did not secure the advantages at this meeting that he was accustomed to expect, but he was the only one of the 'Big Three' to remain in power following the end of the war.

and inspiring oratory, and the King, with his calm dignity, complemented each other perfectly to epitomize Britain's war-time spirit.

In December 1941 the Japanese forced the United States into the war by attacking the American Fleet at Pearl Harbour. The involvement of the United States gave the Allies the long-term advantage in resources and man-power, and although victory was still years and not months away, by June 1943 Rommel had surrendered and the King was able to visit the troops in North Africa. George VI, who was indifferent to his own personal safety, had been longing to visit the troops in action before this but was only too aware that should he be captured by the enemy it would do the Allied cause inestimable harm. He had therefore allowed himself to be dissuaded from visits to troops abroad, although he had been tireless in his morale-boosting visits to camps within the British Isles. The visit to North Africa was an opportunity to meet and talk with the generals, and with Eisenhower in particular, and also to let the troops know personally what their efforts had meant to the country.

After this the King went on to Malta, which had suffered terribly and which he had, in a unique gesture, awarded the George Cross. Although Malta was less than one hundred miles from the enemy forces in Sicily the King, who understood perfectly the psychological effect which his presence would have, insisted on making the journey. Back in England he wrote to Queen Mary:

The real gem of my tour was my visit to Malta. I had set my heart on that and it was not difficult to persuade the Naval and Air C-in-Cs of its importance or of its effect on the island itself. The question was which was the safest route, by sea or by air. I knew there was a risk in any case but it was worth taking. So I went by sea and by night. I shall never forget the sight of entering the Grand Harbour at 8.30 am on a lovely sunny day, and seeing the people cheering from every vantage view-point, while we were still some way off. Then later, when we anchored inside, hearing the cheers of the people which brought a lump to my throat, knowing what they had suffered from six months' constant bombing.

In June 1944 the Allied Armies landed in northern France. Churchill wanted to watch the D-Day landings from one of the Allied ships, and typically the King was determined to join him. His advisers were appalled, and commonsense quickly prevailed, but it was the King himself who had to intervene to prevent Churchill from being present at the culmination of everything he had worked for. He wrote to him:

I have been thinking a great deal of our conversation yesterday, and I have come to the conclusion that it would not be right for either you or me to be where we planned on D-Day. I don't think I need emphasize what it would mean to me personally, and to the whole Allied cause if at this juncture a chance bomb, torpedo or even a mine should remove you from the scene; equally a change of sovereign at this moment would be a serious matter for the country and Empire. We should both, I know, love to be there, but in all seriousness I would ask you to reconsider your plan.

D-Day proved the final turning-point in the war. Ten days afterwards it was possible for the King to visit the beaches to decorate the soldiers, and it was even possible for Montgomery to take him

Ten days after D-Day the King toured the invasion beaches.

inland to watch the action from a distance. In July he visited the troops in Italy, a gesture which was greatly appreciated, for Alexander's army felt that in the excitement of D-Day landings their own efforts had been forgotten. Nevertheless, the war dragged on in Europe for nearly a year, and Germany launched a new type of attack on London, the v-1 and v-2 pilotless bombers. The King and Churchill had to eat their Tuesday lunches in the Buckingham Palace air-raid shelter. One of the v-1s made a direct hit on the Guards' Chapel in Wellington Barracks not far from the Palace, and several of the King's personal friends were killed. Like many of the British people, the King had lost both friends and relatives in the war, including his younger brother Prince George, Duke of Kent, who was killed on a flying mission to Iceland in 1942.

When VE Day came, on 8 May 1945, the government was already as concerned with plans for post-war construction as with running the war itself. Although Japan had not yet been defeated, for most of Britain, except those with relatives still fighting in Burma, the war was over. It was decided that the coalition government had served its purpose, and a General Election was held in the summer. To many people's surprise the Conservatives, with Churchill as their leader, did not get a majority, partly because the Labour party's plans for a new type of society appeared attractive to a country tired of deprivation, and also, perhaps unfairly, because Churchill, who had led the country through the war, now seemed too closely associated with all that it had entailed. The mood which brought the Labour Party to power was one which demanded a fresh start in every aspect of the country's life and therefore one which could well have been totally in tune with a demand for a republican form of government. Yet Britain had probably been closer to republicanism after the First World War. George VI had been a late developer, but during the war he had matured in self-confidence and judgment. By a strange quirk of fate he had turned out to be the right man in the right job at the right time, and so the monarchy emerged from the war a more secure institution than it had been at its outbreak.

But if the monarchy was still secure, it was no longer a source of real political power. This was more apparent under a Socialist government than it had ever been. Yet the opportunity remained for the monarch to discuss and advise on policy, and at the very outset of Attlee's administration George VI did just that on a matter about which he felt very strongly, foreign policy. When Clement Attlee told the King that he intended to give Hugh Dalton the highly influential post of Foreign Secretary, 'I disagreed with him', the King wrote later, 'and said that foreign affairs was the most important subject at the moment and I hoped he would make Mr Bevin take it.' At the Yalta conference in February 1945 it had begun to be apparent that Russia was determined to go her own way and to grab what advantage she could from the defeat of Germany. George VI had always been suspicious of Russia and frightened of Communism, and the establishment of what Churchill was later to call 'the Iron Curtain' showed that he had been right in his suspicions. Bevin, unlike Dalton,

VE Day, the end of the war for Britain. The Royal Family with Winston Churchill on the balcony of Buckingham Palace.

was a man whose own suspicions of Russia's motives and desire for a special relationship with the United States to counteract Communism accorded well with George VI's own opinions. In the event, their common attitude turned out to have been well founded, and Attlee did not regret listening to the King's advice on that occasion, for Bevin became an astute Foreign Secretary and, given Britain's relative weakness, achieved as much as could have been expected.

Naturally George VI had been sorry to see Churchill go. The two men had been friends as well as colleagues. In his farewell letter the King wrote: 'For myself personally I regret what has happened more than perhaps anyone else. I shall miss your counsel to me more than I can say. But please remember that as a friend I hope we shall be able to meet at intervals ... believe me, I am yours very sincerely, and gratefully G.R.I. [George, *Rex, Imperator* – George, King, Emperor].' The King and Attlee were never on the same easy terms, although they had got to know each other quite well when Attlee had acted as Deputy Prime Minister during Churchill's absences abroad. 'My new government is not too easy and the people are rather difficult to talk to,' the King wrote to his brother.

Attlee's government ushered in a period of rapid social reform virtually creating the Welfare State in a few short years. George VI was certainly no radical: he had all the conservative instincts of his class and would have preferred more gradual change. Yet his involvement before the war with the IWS and the boys' camps

Left The King and Queen pictured during their tour of South Africa in 1947. It was an important tour which may have helped to keep South Africa in the Commonwealth a little longer.

Below The King and Queen, with the Princesses Elizabeth and Margaret (seated in the car) are given an enthusiastic welcome by the white South Africans.

indicated that he had liberal views and was fully aware of the need for reforms. It was therefore not as difficult as might have been expected for him to support his Labour Prime Minister as he had supported his Conservative Prime Ministers, and in doing so he increased the security of the monarchy as an institution by scotching the fear that a king and a Socialist government could not work well together.

While his role in home affairs was almost entirely passive, the King was still able to make a positive contribution in foreign policy. This has always been an aspect of government in which the sovereign is expected to take a particular interest, a notion left over from the time when foreign policy was largely a dynastic matter concerned with alliances between different royal families. Additionally the King and Bevin got on well together: Bevin was one of the few ministers who took the trouble to discuss affairs with the King. Britain was at a crucial stage in her foreign policy, for it was the beginning of a long period of adjustment to the fact that she no longer commanded the resources to be a super power on a par with Russia and the United States. What is more, the Empire which for the last hundred years had helped to bear the cost of Britain's policies was now coming to an end. A Commonwealth of independent states bound together by mutual history and a desire to retain their access to the financial resources of the City of London, which was still one of the major financial centres of the world, was evolving to take its place.

One of the Dominions which was showing signs of wanting to break away altogether was South Africa, where the Afrikaans-speaking Nationalist party was growing in strength. George VI, anxious to preserve every possible aspect of Britain's status as a world power, agreed to visit South Africa. This tour coincided with the bad winter of 1947, and the King was extremely sensitive to accusations that the Royal Family had chosen to sun itself in Africa rather than share the deprivation at home. Nevertheless, he was determined to make the visit before the South African election in 1948, and the tour, although it did not prevent a Nationalist victory at the polls, did show that the King himself was still personally popular. So the tour may have helped to keep South Africa in the Commonwealth a little longer, when it had been feared that an Afrikaner government would take her out immediately.

In the immediate post-war period the future of India was of paramount concern. India was clearly determined to throw off direct British rule, and the question of independence was complicated by the fact that the Hindus and Muslims were unable to reach a peaceful

compromise between themselves. George VI was doubly anxious over the future of India, for not only might it decrease Britain's prestige if she opted out of the Commonwealth altogether but it was thought it would not be possible for Britain to leave without terrible bloodshed resulting as the Hindus and Muslims fought for control. Eventually a compromise was reached in 1947 by partitioning the sub-continent into two countries, Hindu India and Muslim Pakistan. The man appointed as Viceroy of India to oversee the transition to independence was the King's cousin Earl Mountbatten of Burma. Mountbatten was given virtually a free hand to bring India to independence, and it made it a good deal easier for the King to come to terms with losing the title 'Emperor of India', with all that it implied in lost British prestige, knowing that the British Raj was to be brought to a close by a member of his own family.

Earl Mountbatten had proved himself both a brilliant strategist and a canny negotiator during the war in the Far East. His equal success in India can be judged by the fact that he was asked to stay on

The King and Queen at Balmoral.

Above George VI and Queen Mary at the Presentation of the Horses, Buckingham Palace. Princess Elizabeth is standing on the left.

Right The King and Queen at Buckingham Palace, 1948, on the occasion of their silver wedding anniversary.

A firework display for the Festival of Britain on the south bank of the Thames in 1951. The Festival, a celebration of 'fun, fantasy and colour' was a sign that the years of austerity were at last over.

as India's first Governor General once she had achieved Dominion status. The actual Head of State of India (and of Pakistan) was to be a President, unlike Britain's older Dominions such as Canada, which accepted the King as their Head of State as well as Head of the Commonwealth. The King's contribution at this time to the creation of a new concept of Commonwealth was his readiness to accept the notion that India owed him allegiance as Head of the Commonwealth but not as Emperor or King of India. By agreeing to the new formula, George VI helped make it possible for the Commonwealth to retain many countries which would otherwise have left altogether. The concept of a republic being a member of the Commonwealth, and in that capacity owing allegiance to someone who also happens to be the British sovereign, is now totally accepted (there are twenty-one republics which are member states), but in 1947 it came as a revolutionary new idea.

In 1948 there came the first indications of the King's ill health. He developed circulation trouble and in March 1949 was forced to cancel a planned tour of Australia and New Zealand. He had an operation which was fairly successful, although he was told that if a second thrombosis developed it might well prove fatal. His health, which was never very good, had been impaired by the stresses of the war years. It was further damaged by heavy smoking, just as his father's and grandfather's had been. In 1951 the King fulfilled a busy schedule which included the successful Festival of Britain. Then he became ill again, this time with influenza, but further examination revealed that he was suffering from lung cancer. It is doubtful if the King ever realized the exact nature of his illness, although he had an operation for the removal of his left lung in September 1951. The operation appeared to be successful, and he recovered enough to spend an enjoyable family Christmas at Sandringham. Nevertheless he had to rest most of the time, which made him extremely impatient with his own apparent inability to get back to normal, and the Christmas radio broadcast was recorded a sentence at a time to minimize the strain on his voice. On 30 January 1952 the whole family went to see *South Pacific* at Drury Lane. It was the night before Princess Elizabeth and her husband, Prince Philip, were due to fly to Africa to undertake a tour which George VI was too ill to make himself. The next day the King saw them off at the airport looking tired and strained, before returning to Sandringham to continue his convalescence.

On 5 February he went out to shoot hares and had a successful day. That night he died peacefully in his sleep.

George VI was genuinely mourned by the whole nation for, in spite of the inauspicious start to his reign, he had slowly won the respect and affection of the people. He undoubtedly had good personal qualities – he was devoutly religious, loving to his family and intensely loyal to his country. Yet had it not been for the war he would probably have been remembered as a worthy but dull man. As it was, the qualities which he possessed made him the ideal monarch during those momentous years. At that time his dignity and quiet determination, together with a sincere desire to endure everything with the people, made him the epitome of everything worth fighting for. His inexperience in politics scarcely mattered, for the situation was entirely novel, and in retrospect it seems doubtful whether Britain in the Second World War could have had a better king than the man who so unwillingly came to the throne in 1936.

The body of George VI lying in state at Westminster Hall. On the coffin are the imperial crown and the Queen Mother's wreath.

CHAPTER FIVE

Elizabeth II

When news of the death of George VI reached his daughter, the twenty-six-year-old Princess Elizabeth was already deputizing for him, making the tour of East Africa and Australia that her father had been too ill to undertake. Prince Philip broke the news to her, and though her entourage tried not to intrude on her grief as a private individual, it was inevitable that now she was Queen even coping with this shock had to take second place to her duty as Head of State. Almost immediately the question of what she should be called had to be decided. Several of her predecessors, including her father, had been crowned using names other than the Christian names to which they were accustomed; the 'new' names, with their historic connotations, were considered more fitting to the monarch's status. When asked what name she would use, the Queen chose unhesitatingly to go on using her own name. So it was as 'Elizabeth II' that she flew back to London to be met by Churchill and her other Ministers of State. The photographs of the pale and tense young woman dressed in black (a set of mourning clothes is always included in the sovereign's luggage, even when there is no imminent death in the family) certainly aroused the sympathy of the public. George VI had proved an immensely popular monarch, despite the inauspicious circumstances of his accession. Now the people of post-war Britain were keen to show their enthusiasm for his daughter and to see in her the symbol of a new and better world; in fact many newspapers spoke of 'a second Elizabethan age', recalling the nation's success and prosperity under Elizabeth I four hundred years earlier.

Elizabeth had been born on 21 April 1926, at 21 Bruton Street, the London home of her mother's parents, the Earl and Countess of Strathmore. She was christened by the Archbishop of York – her father was Duke of York at the time – and given the names 'Elizabeth Alexandra Mary' after her mother, her great-grandmother (who had died the previous year) and her grandmother, the then Queen. She and her sister, Princess Margaret, who was born four years later, were brought up in a relatively informal way for children in their position. George VI had suffered greatly from his mother's apparent indifference to him (and indeed to all her children) and from his father's rigid discipline and lack of any outward show of affection: he and his wife therefore gave their children much more of their time than might have been expected of a royal Duke and Duchess.

Opposite Queen Elizabeth II.

Above The Green Drawing Room, Buckingham Palace.

Interestingly George V and Queen Mary, who had been so unbending with their own children, doted on their grand-daughters, and 'Lilibet' as Elizabeth called herself, was a great favourite. For a while the family lived at 145 Piccadilly, then in 1931 they moved to Royal Lodge, Windsor (now one of the homes of the Queen Mother), and, untroubled by intimations of the future, led the type of country life which all four of them found so compatible. This period of relative obscurity and family life was in many ways the happiest time for them. In spite of their success in the role, neither George VI nor his daughter would have chosen to be monarch. The Queen once remarked to her riding-instructor that given a choice she would have preferred to be a lady living in the country with lots of horses and dogs, and her chosen leisure activities of horse-breeding and racing, walking, stalking and riding, bear this out.

The abdication crisis came therefore as an unwelcome upheaval to the Duke of York and his family. Nine-year-old Princess Elizabeth became Heir Presumptive to her father, and great thought now had to be given to her education and preparation for her likely role as queen. Like most girls of an aristocratic background, Elizabeth and her sister had been educated at home by governesses. The idea was mooted that Elizabeth should be sent to boarding-school, but George VI turned it down. He felt that a girl who would one day be queen should not mix

with other girls at school. Clearly the Queen, who has always, even after years of experience, seemed rather shy in company, has found this decision a disadvantage. It is significant that her own children were all sent away to school, and all of them seem very confident and at ease with other people.

Having made the decision not to send his heir to school, George VI was determined to make sure that she was not as ill-equipped as he had been for the demanding job of monarch. He could not, and did not, appreciate how greatly the demands of that role were to change during the war and its aftermath, but he did make sure that she became proficient in French, a useful language for international diplomacy, and that as well as lessons in such ladylike subjects as music and drawing, she also got a good grounding in more practical disciplines, such as constitutional history. As soon as Elizabeth was old enough to benefit from the training, he initiated her into the mysteries of the red dispatch-boxes in which the monarch's official papers are kept, and did his best to ensure that she knew what the monarch's role in the constitution entailed.

This may seem an obvious preparation for the future, but it contrasted markedly with the attitude of previous monarchs to their heirs. Queen Victoria had pointedly kept the future Edward VII well away from anything to do with the day-to-day workings of his future job, and, more recently, George V had shown a great reluctance to help the Prince of Wales to understand the intricacies of the constitutional monarch's position other than as a good public relations man. So, on her father's death, Princess Elizabeth probably had a greater understanding of what was expected of her than many of her recent predecessors and, in spite of a naturally retiring nature,

Right The Entrée Stairs, Buckingham Palace.

was better equipped to cope with her situation. Perhaps what stood her in greatest stead at that time was the marked sense of duty which came naturally to her and which had been encouraged and strengthened not only by her father but by her grandmother, Queen Mary, whose influence over her grand-daughter had been considerable. The sight of this formidable old lady curtseying to her grand-daughter when she returned from Kenya on 7 February must have brought home the implications of her status very clearly to the new Queen.

During the war years, when their father and mother stayed on in London, Princess Elizabeth and Princess Margaret lived at Windsor and spent occasional periods at Balmoral. When, during the early part of the war, it seemed that Britain might be invaded, it was seriously suggested that Elizabeth and her sister be sent to the United States, not only for their own personal safety but to ensure that the heir to the throne remained free. The Princesses, said the Queen, would not leave without their mother; she would not leave without her husband, and the King would never leave. The idea was quickly dropped. This reply typified the spirit and personal courage of the Royal Family which is one important reason why they continue to inspire the type of loyalty whch is rarely given to an elected Head of State. It also typified the family feeling with which people are able to identify and which is another strength of the British monarchy as it has developed in the twentieth century. Princess Elizabeth's life during the greater part of the war was therefore quiet and secluded. When she became eighteen, at her own insistence she entered National Service, joining the ATS as a second subaltern in 1945.

Like other parents during the war, George VI and his wife regretted the way in which war had taken from their children a large part of the carefree period of growing up.

On the night the war in Europe ended, the two Princesses were allowed out incognito, escorted by two Guards officers, to join the enthusiastic thousands who filled the London streets and gathered round Buckingham Palace. As life returned slowly to a more normal pattern, the nineteen-year-old Princess was photographed going to dances and dinner parties, and the inevitable speculation began about whom and when she would marry. However the decision was already as good as made, as the Press soon discovered, for like so many other young women during the war her anxiety had been focused on one particular person.

Lieutenant Philip Mountbatten RN, as he was at the end of the war, was related to the British Royal Family on both his mother's and his father's side. Although his father was Prince Andrew of Greece, the brother of the King of the Hellenes, his family was Danish in origin and related to Elizabeth because the Danish Prince who had become King of Greece was the brother of Edward VII's wife Alexandra. Philip's mother, Alice, was the daughter of one of Queen Victoria's grand-daughters and Louis of Battenberg. The Battenbergs had adopted an anglicized version of their name, Mountbatten, and it was therefore his mother's maiden name that Prince Philip chose to be

Opposite Princess Elizabeth and Lieutenant Philip Mountbatten RN on their wedding day, 20 November 1947. The occasion provided the first royal pageantry seen since the Second World War and it was a tonic to the nation.

Queen Elizabeth II in the robes of the Most Noble Order of the Garter.

known by. When the marriage of his parents broke up, his father went to live in the South of France while his mother founded a religious order in Greece. It was the English Mountbattens who therefore provided Philip with a home and stability, and his mother's brother Lord Louis Mountbatten was particularly close to him. They sent him to Cheam preparatory school in England, and then to Germany, where the famous German educationalist Kurt Hahn had started a school at Schloss Salem, the home of the Margrave of Baden who was married to one of Philip's four older sisters. Hahn, who was persecuted in Nazi Germany because of his Jewish origins, came to Britain, where he had many influential admirers and supporters, including Ramsay MacDonald, and re-established a similar school at Gordonstoun in Scotland, to which Prince Philip was sent. He did exceptionally well there, for Hahn's school was particularly intended to cater for boys like him whose background made it likely that they would have an influential role to play in life. The emphasis was, and still is, on self-sufficiency and enterprise and on inculcating a firm sense of duty in people who might otherwise be tempted to enjoy the privileges of their station in life without any corresponding sense of 'noblesse oblige'. Much of the time was spent in outdoor pursuits to encourage a sense of adventure and physical courage. The regime and the principles suited Prince Philip well and stood him in good stead in later life, although in some ways an education which fits people for leadership, as did Philip's school and his later naval training at Dartmouth, may be a disadvantage to someone whose eventual role is to take second place. Some of Prince Philip's inevitable frustration at having always to be in a slightly subservient position may well be due to this. On the other hand the ideals have helped him come to terms with his position, and the lifetime's interest in sport of every kind has given him an outlet for much of his untapped energy.

George VI and Queen Elizabeth approved of their daughter's choice of husband but, feeling that she was still rather young for such a momentous decision, and conscious of the fact that she had not met many other young men, they postponed any announcement until after a four-month tour of Africa, to see whether their affection for each other would outlast this final separation as well as Philip's many absences throughout the war. It was during this tour that Elizabeth celebrated her twenty-first birthday and made the famous radio broadcast to the young people of the Empire and Commonwealth in which she dedicated her life to the service of the people:

If we all go forward together, with unswerving faith, a high courage and a quiet heart, we shall be able to make of this ancient Commonwealth which we all love so dearly, an even grander thing – more free, more prosperous, more happy and a more powerful influence for good in the world – than it has been in the greatest days of our forefathers. To accomplish that, we must give nothing less than the whole of ourselves. I declare before you that my whole life, whether it be long or short, shall be devoted to your service and the service of our great imperial family to which we all belong.

It showed a shrewd understanding, perhaps on her own part, certainly on that of the Royal Family's advisers, of the future emphasis

Queen Elizabeth II returns from her coronation in the gold state coach, 1953.

of the role of monarch as a unifying symbol for a Commonwealth united by its own free will, not by any pressure from Britain. The additional emphasis on the sense of duty, which the Princess felt at the time and later as monarch, was undoubtedly her own. Whatever reservations critics have of the constitutional monarchy as a system of government, the dedication of Elizabeth II to her work has never been in doubt.

Her wedding to Prince Philip on 20 November 1947 in Westminster Abbey gave her an insight into the psychological lift which the grander moments of royal pageantry can inspire. Then, as on later occasions, there were those who carped at the expense, although in fact most of the wedding expenses were paid by George VI out of the privy purse. Yet as the hundreds of wedding gifts from ordinary people poured into Buckingham Palace, it was obvious that most had the same attitude as Winston Churchill who said: 'Millions will welcome this joyous event as a flash of colour on the hard road we have to travel.' Moreover for foreign observers it was a clear sign that Britain was getting back to normal, despite the evidence of the devastating bombing of her cities and the immediate post-war difficulties which made rationing a continuing necessity.

For two years the couple lived at Buckingham Palace before moving to Clarence House. Prince Philip, who had found simply being Princess Elizabeth's husband and escort an unsatisfying way of life, resumed his active naval career in October of the same year and joined the First Mediterranean Fleet based in Malta. The Princess joined her husband as often as she could and usually stayed with Earl and Countess Mountbatten. Prince Charles was born on 14 November 1948 and Princess Anne on 15 August 1950. Even in the twentieth century this guarantee of the continuity of the dynasty was important to the stability of the monarchy. It was particularly important so soon after the upheaval of the abdication, which had shown how greatly the effectiveness of the monarchy depended on the character and strengths of the monarch himself and on the smoothness of continuity.

The short period as a naval wife came to a close as the health of George VI, which had always been poor, began obviously to deteriorate. Princess Elizabeth took over an increasing number of his formal duties. In 1949, for example, she stood in for him at the Trooping of the Colour; in 1951 she undertook a strenuous tour of Canada, accompanied by the Duke of Edinburgh. This was followed by a brief visit to Washington, where she met President Truman. After the visit, Truman sent George VI a telegram with the message, 'As one father to another we can be very proud of our daughters.' This was the first of countless similar meetings with the world's great statesmen which were to give her a breadth of experience and network of personal contacts second to none, a valuable asset to her governments and one unique to the monarch, who has the greater part of a lifetime to build up such a network in a way not possible for a politician elected for a limited period.

So Elizabeth II came to the throne better trained and more

The coronation in Westminster Abbey, 2 June 1953, was the first time a coronation service had ever been televized.

Queen Elizabeth looking radiant during her tour of the United States in July 1976.

experienced than any of her immediate predecessors for the task ahead. She had also the advantage of a supportive family, the value of which her own mother's work on behalf of George VI had made abundantly clear. Her accession coincided with a period of full employment, revived prosperity and stability. The new Queen was welcomed enthusiastically as a symbol of this optimistic era, and her coronation the following year (2 June 1953) was the epitome of the pageantry of which the British Royal Family is capable and of the emotions, particularly the sense of national unity, which such occasions can tap and foster. Elizabeth II's coronation was better organized and stage-managed than any before. Preparation took months under the direction of the hereditary Earl Marshal, the Duke of Norfolk. The cost was something approaching £2,000,000, and the schedule was calculated to within thirty seconds. Contrary to popular belief there is no rigid ceremonial laid down for the coronation of the monarch, although of course certain elements, particularly the focal points of the anointing with oil and placing the crown on the head of the sovereign, have always been present since the original pre-Conquest ceremony. Elizabeth's coronation exploited every possible aspect of the symbolism inherent in this ceremony.

In addition to the traditional regalia representing such kingly virtues as Faith, Mercy and Justice, the Queen's coronation dress itself was symbolic, incorporating into its embroidery the emblems of the Dominions: Australia, New Zealand, India and Canada. A pleasing coincidence which provided its own element of symbolism was the news on the morning of the coronation that a New Zealander, Edmund Hillary, with John Hunt and Sherpa Tensing, had finally conquered Everest, the world's highest mountain. The *Daily Express* carried the now-famous headline 'All this and Everest Too'.

The coronation had brilliantly epitomized one aspect of monarchy which had always been significant and which still matters in the twentieth century – its symbolism and the expression of that symbolism in ceremony and pageantry. A sideline of the ceremonial has of course been its attractiveness to tourists, themselves a twentieth-century phenomenon, and this has proved a minor though valuable new aspect of the monarchy's role.

However, simply existing, however impressively is no longer considered a sufficient justification in itself for the monarchy. Elizabeth II, by instinct or calculated judgment immediately became involved in what has become, during her reign, an ever more important part of the job – to be seen; and not just in this country but equally importantly in the countries of the Commonwealth and what remains of the old Empire. Immediately after the coronation, the Queen and the Duke of Edinburgh toured the British Isles and reviewed the three armed forces. On 23 November they embarked on an arduous tour of the Commonwealth. In six months the Queen and her husband visited Canada, Bermuda, Jamaica, Fiji, Tonga, New Zealand, Australia, the Cocos Islands, Ceylon, Aden, Uganda, Malta and Gibraltar. The enthusiastic reception she received confirmed the inestimable value of these personal appearances, as her Uncle David had found on the many tours he undertook as Prince of Wales. The by now traditional Christmas radio broadcast was made from New Zealand that year, and in it the Queen spoke specifically of the Commonwealth which was fast evolving from the British Empire: 'It is an entirely new conception ... the most effective and progressive association of peoples which history has yet seen.' Yet again she was able to build upon the personal contacts she made. One particularly close association which began with this tour was with Robert Menzies, who remained a staunch supporter of Australia's links with Britain until his death in 1977. In his reply to the Queen's speech opening the Australian Parliament, a speech which had emphasized the brotherhood of the peoples of the Commonwealth, he said of the Queen: 'She has, I believe, helped us to understand more perfectly that humility and pride can co-exist; that, under a queen like her, subjecthood is no mark of inferiority but is in itself a title of honour.' During the constitutional crisis in Australia in 1976, when the Queen's Governor General, Sir John Kerr, dismissed the Prime Minister, Gough Whitlam, and caused many Australians to call for Australia's complete independence of interference from Britain, Robert Menzies was quick to defend the British link. A similar situation arose in 1978 during the Queen's visit to Edmonton to open the Commonwealth Games. This inevitably provoked those who want to renounce Dominion status for unqualified independence (and in particular those who want a separate French-speaking state) to call for an immediate change of constitution. On this occasion it was John Diefenbaker, by now a Canadian 'elder statesman' and long-standing acquaintance of the Queen, who spoke up strongly in defence of the *status quo*.

On the final stage of the 1953–4 tour, the Queen and Duke of Edinburgh were joined by Prince Charles and Princess Anne, who had travelled to meet them at Tobruk in the new royal yacht, *Britannia*. The *Britannia* has since been frequently used for royal tours. It enables the Queen to entertain foreign statesmen and officials on British territory even while abroad. During the Silver Jubilee visit to the troubled province of Ulster in August 1977, its use avoided a potentially embarrassing situation: the Queen travelled to Belfast on *Britannia* and stayed on the yacht, which avoided her having to employ obtrusively heavy security, which would have been necessary had she stayed somewhere on shore. She was also able to entertain prominent Ulster men and women, such as the leaders of the Peace Movement, Mairead Corrigan and Betty Williams, and also to increase the impression of normality by bringing her two younger sons, Prince Andrew and Prince Edward.

After the first twenty-five years of her reign, it has become the accepted norm for the monarch to be constantly travelling and always on display in a way that would have been totally alien to as recent a monarch as George V. Elizabeth II has strengthened the monarchy by her willingness to accept this inevitable new state of affairs gracefully. She has visited every Commonwealth country at

Queen Elizabeth and Prince Philip sightseeing during one of many world tours.

The Queen and
Prince Philip are
greeted by a tribal
chief at a durbar in
Sierra Leone during
their triumphant
tour of West Africa
in 1961.

The Queen atop an
elephant in
Katmandu during
the royal visit to
India in 1961.

Right The Queen's tour of Japan in May 1975. There was obviously delight on both sides of this encounter.

Below The Queen shows intense interest in a ceremonial dragon at a street festival held in her honour.

The Queen Mother arrives at Covent Garden for a gala performance.

least once, and most other foreign countries as well. In 1972 she visited Yugoslavia, the first official visit by any British monarch to a Communist country. She has now got the business of travel down to a fine art, even to the minor but important details such as taking her own supply of bottled drinking-water and her own pillow wherever she goes.

An important factor to be born in mind in the meticulous planning which goes into these foreign tours, and indeed an important part of her role as a twentieth-century monarch constantly being photographed and filmed, is the question of what the Queen wears. Her dresser, 'Bobo' MacDonald, is a power to be reckoned with in the royal household (some writers have implied that she is the Queen's only confidante outside her immediate family). She has been with the Queen since she was a girl and has a very important task in making sure that the Queen is always immaculately and appropriately dressed whatever the occasion. The royal dress designers have the task of combining her dual roles as an object of 'glamour' who is also the epitome of the dignity of the state she represents. Although her publicity and Press coverage are greater than that of any film star, it would not be appropriate for her to dress in an ostentatious way.

The 'glamorous' side of her role is reflected in the elaborate evening-gowns she wears on formal occasions such as the State Opening of Parliament, and in the jewellery and tiaras which she and other female members of the Royal Family wear. As this style of dress becomes increasingly outdated, the impact of it increases. When she was a young and beautiful woman, the Queen easily stood out in a crowd even when formal evening-wear was still worn by everyone. Now that she is middle-aged and formal evening-wear is a rarity, she still manages to stand out because she is usually the only woman dressed in this rather outdated way.

On less formal public occasions, however, the Queen's dress has often been a subject of criticism. Such criticism is not mere carping for it is evident that what the Queen wears is an integral part of the job she does. On the first occasion she wore spectacles in public (the opening of the 1977 Canadian Parliament), the photograph was on the front page of newspapers around the world. She is undoubtedly very conservative in her choice of clothes, and was so even as a young woman. Often in photographs her outfits seem very dull, though the similarity from year to year, with only minor variations of cut and hemline, does help to create an impression of timelessness which contributes in a small way to the monarchy's great asset of seeming to be the one dependable element in society. However, one of the great features of the Queen's wardrobe which has become more obvious with the advent of colour photography and colour television is the sense of colour that she and her designers have. Her outfits are nearly always in extremely bright, clear shades, such as yellow, turquoise or pink, which means that she is easily recognizable even to an observer catching a quick glimpse of her from the back of the crowd.

Such outfits, as her critics point out, would of course look out of place on the average woman in the street, but they indicate clearly

The Queen Mother, Princess Margaret and Princess Anne attending the Royal Variety Performance which is held each year in honour of the Royal Family.

Right Christmas is always a family affair for the Queen and is spent at Windsor. She is seen here on the steps of St George's Chapel with the Dean of Windsor after Matins on Christmas Day.

Far right The 'glamorous' side of Queen Elizabeth: she is seen here in formal evening-wear, accompanied by President Ford of the United States in 1976.

Above The Duke of Edinburgh at the Royal Windsor Horse Show in 1974.

Opposite Queen Elizabeth at Balmoral, a photograph taken for the royal silver wedding anniversary.

that the Queen and her designers (usually the London couturiers Norman Hartnell and Hardy Amies) understand the function of her clothes better than the fashion journalists who have criticized her. Other factors which have to be taken into consideration are also unlikely to affect the average woman. Her designers must bear in mind that she may occasionally have to ride on an elephant in a particular outfit without appearing in any way undignified! She is constantly getting in and out of cars and on and off boats while all eyes are on her, so her dresses must not ride up and expose more leg than is proper. Even when she is safely sitting, she may be waving, and so her clothes must be cut to take this into account and not ride up or be uncomfortable. They also have to be adaptable to different climates and to the vagaries of the British weather, so coats are made with two matching dresses, one winter-weight and one summer-weight. The Queen may change her outfits six times a day when on a busy foreign tour, so clothes also have to be designed for quick changing and for easy care. Not surprisingly, while off duty, the Queen has always preferred simple, country-style clothes – tweed skirts, arran sweaters, head scarves and sensible shoes.

One reason for the particular care which the Queen has taken with her wardrobe is the fact that, unlike any previous monarch, her every move has been seen by thousands or even millions because of the rapid development of television after the end of the Second World War. This growth in the influence of television has coincided almost exactly with her reign: the coronation was the first major royal event to be televized. At the time, few people owned television sets, and for many their first memory of television is watching the coronation crowded round a set in a public place such as a pub or hotel. Even so early the way in which television imposes its demands was already being felt: the rigorous planning and time-table of the coronation, so unlike the more haphazard ceremonies on previous occasions, was largely in order to simplify matters for the television cameras.

Since George V made his first radio broadcast to the nation the public has become increasingly to expect the Royal Family to be available to them. Once the mystery and prestige of monarchy was increased by its remoteness; now such remoteness is not acceptable either to the British people or to the Commonwealth. To be at ease with the media is now one of the secrets of being a successful monarch. In some ways this has proved Elizabeth II's greatest weakness. She has managed to maintain a careful balance between the dignity of her office and being a public person and available to the media (for example, the television film of the Royal Family at home was made at her instigation in 1969, and in 1977 as part of the Jubilee celebrations she and her family took part in a series of television films about the art treasures in the royal collection), but when she is conscious of performing directly for the cameras, Her Majesty seems very unnatural and awkward and gives an unfortunate impression of being a difficult person to get on with, an impression quite at variance with the one she gives when more relaxed.

In 1957 it was decided to replace the Christmas radio broadcast

The Queen pictured with the Duke of Beaufort and the Duke's hounds, at Badminton.

with a televized speech. For the first few years, until television techniques made pre-recording the normal procedure, this speech was televized live after Christmas lunch and was clearly a great ordeal. The Duke of Edinburgh was also understandably nervous during his first few television appearances but has developed into a more accomplished television personality. Their children have always seemed totally at home as television performers, particularly Prince Charles, who has made numerous appearances, often as a programme presenter or narrator. The ability to use television well and to his own advantage is one of his most useful assets.

Elizabeth II has undoubtedly exploited the rapid technological developments in travel and communications to make herself a familiar figure both in the British Isles and in the Commonwealth. Her power as a symbol and figurehead has been well used, and her personality has proved remarkably sympathetic to a wide range of races and people. By making so much of this aspect of her role, she has compensated for the continuing decrease in the real power of the monarch which was unmistakably evident even during the reign of Queen Victoria. Since the reign of George V, no one has even pretended that the monarch's power exists in any meaningful way. However, the rights of the constitutional monarch to be consulted and to advise do still exist, and Elizabeth II has not neglected them. Inevitably, as her experience has grown, she has been listened to with more respect by her Prime Ministers, probably most of all by one of the most recent, Harold Wilson. This is interesting as, being a Socialist, the reverse was to be expected. Surprisingly their relationship was so good that on his resignation the Queen made him a Knight of the Garter, one of the few honours still in her personal gift. For his part he praised her political sagacity in his memoirs and emphasized the value of her knowledge and experience to her Prime Ministers.

No one believes that a British monarch in the last quarter of the twentieth century can impose any sort of political decision on the government. Winston Churchill, Elizabeth II's first Prime Minister, in fact described the value of having a monarch above political faction:

In our island, by trial and error and by perseverance across the centuries, we have found out a very good plan. Here it is. The Queen can do no wrong; and advisers can be changed as often as the people like to use their right for that purpose. A great battle is won; crowds cheer the Queen. What goes wrong is carted away with the politicians responsible.

Nonetheless, the Queen has considerable influence, not just with politicians at home but with people abroad, few of whom are not flattered by a personal invitation from her. In cultivating these personal contacts and smoothing the path for the government's foreign relations, Elizabeth II is building on the precedent set by her great-grandfather, Edward VII, who saw the value of putting his influence and prestige to work as an ambassador and who made a major contribution to the Anglo–French *entente cordiale* prior to the First World War.

In 1956 the Suez crisis, when Britain and France tried to prevent

Egypt by force from nationalizing the Suez Canal which was so vital to their links with the Indian Ocean, caused tremendous hostility towards Britain. Not only was she trying to impose the sort of gun-boat diplomacy which had ceased to be relevant in the post-imperial era but she had shown that she no longer had the strength to make such intervention effective. Many of the new Commonwealth nations were deeply offended by the apparent return to imperialist attitudes. Canada was strongly opposed to the British action, as was the United States, which quickly intervened, along with the Soviet Union, to enforce a humiliating cease-fire on Britain and France.

The Queen and Prince Philip stop to enjoy a conversation during a ride in Windsor Great Park.

143

There is no evidence that the Queen made any attempt to intervene in the handling of the Suez crisis. What she did do was to use her personal influence to the utmost to repair the damage done to Britain's relations with the Commonwealth and with her most powerful ally, the United States. In 1957 she went to Canada, where she made a television broadcast to the nation and opened the Canadian Parliament in her capacity as Queen of Canada, thereby emphasizing Canada's ties with Britain. She then went to Washington, where she met President Eisenhower and initiated a lasting friendship between them. In June 1959 she returned to Canada yet again for a two-month tour which included opening the St Lawrence Seaway jointly with President Eisenhower, and in September 1959 the American President was entertained at Balmoral, the Queen's private Scottish residence.

Each visit that the Queen pays abroad and each time she entertains a foreign Head of State furthers good relations between Britain and the rest of the world. Several of these occasions exemplify the contribution which the monarchy still makes even though its constitutional importance is now so curtailed. In 1965 the Queen paid an official visit to West Germany, the first visit since the end of the war. She was received with enormous enthusiasm by the German people, and the visit provoked little hostile reaction at home. It had tested the ground and it opened the way for Britain eventually to enter the EEC, of which Germany is a leading member. In 1978 she paid another visit to West Germany, and once again the enthusiasm of the German people was overwhelming – some newspapers even going so far as to call her 'Our Queen'. While the visit could not have quite the significance of the first State Visit thirteen years earlier, *The Times*' correspondent wrote: 'The comments of onlookers make it clear that her walks among the crowds had far greater impact on ordinary Germans than years of work by diplomats.'

During this visit the Queen demonstrated yet another role of the monarchy; to clarify the government's policy in public. This she did at a speech to a twenty-five-thousand-strong crowd in Berlin, when she reaffirmed Britain's intentions to fulfill obligations to West Berlin, saying: 'Berlin and Britain are joined by a multitude of ties, of interest, of the mind and of the heart – the basis for a confident and shared future.' Three months later the British government announced plans to increase the size of the British Army of the Rhine by allowing the Army to recruit four thousand more men.

In 1976 the Queen visited the United States for the bicentennial celebrations of independence from Britain. Britain and the United States had each been preoccupied with its own individual problems during the early 1970s and with inflation in particular. Britain's resulting defence cuts had alarmed the United States, which began to fear that Britain would not be able to meet her NATO obligations. The success of Elizabeth II's historic visit was an important counterbalance to the cooling of the relationship between the two countries. In a speech at Independence Hall, Philadelphia, she made the

The royal tour of the USA in 1976. This important visit was to celebrate two hundred years of independence for America.

soothing conciliatory statement: 'We lost the American colonies because we lacked that statesmanship to know the right time and manner of yielding what is impossible to keep.'

Queen Elizabeth and Prince Philip with the American President Gerald Ford and his wife Betty during the US tour.

While nurturing the 'special relationship' with the United States and preparing the ground for Britain's entry into the Common Market with visits to member countries (Denmark in 1960, Italy in 1961, the Netherlands in 1962, Germany in 1965, Belgium in 1966, France in 1972) and entertaining their Heads of State in this country, especially just before Britain's final acceptance into the Community (in 1972 the Heads of State of the Netherlands, Luxembourg and Germany all visited Britain), the Queen was also able to serve government policy in relation to the Commonwealth.

Commonwealth countries had viewed Britain's inexorable moves towards Common Market membership with alarm, especially while the fervent pro-European Prime Minister Edward Heath was in office between 1970 and 1974. The Queen's visits to Commonwealth countries began again with renewed vigour after a break since the tour of the West Indies in 1966. Between 1970 and 1975 Elizabeth II visited Canada five times, New Zealand twice, Australia three times and also Tonga, Kenya, the New Hebrides, the British Solomon Islands, Papua, New Guinea, Bermuda, Barbados, the Bahamas and Hong Kong.

In 1963 she was able to put her political experience to more direct use when Harold Macmillan, the Conservative Prime Minister,

Queen Elizabeth on 'walkabout', at the Hutchestown Gorbals multi-storey flats, Scotland, 1972. The Queen's decision to adopt this new technique of the walkabout has proved immensely popular in the 1970s.

resigned because of ill health. His resignation came at a difficult time because the Conservative Party, although it still commanded a majority in the House of Commons, had been seriously compromized by the Profumo scandal earlier that year. (John Profumo, Secretary for War, had lied to the Commons about his involvement with a prostitute, Christine Keeler. The scandal was more serious because Miss Keeler was also involved with a Russian Embassy official at the same time, and national security was considered to have been put at risk as much as moral rectitude.) When the Prime Minister of a party with a Commons majority resigns, one of the monarch's few remaining constitutional rights is to send for the man whom he or she thinks is most likely to form a government. This means in effect that it is the new leader of the party with a majority in the Commons who is invited to form a government. The Queen's relationship with Harold Macmillan had been extremely good. When he resigned she wrote to him:

For me it means that for the greater part of my reign you have not only been in charge of Britain's policies but you have been my guide and supporter through the mazes of international affairs and my instructor in many vital matters relating to our constitution and to the political and social life of my people.

There is, therefore, no question of your successor, however admirable he may be, being able to perform exactly those services which you have given so generously and for which I am so deeply grateful.

Harold Macmillan was opposed to the idea of R.A. Butler's succeeding him as Prime Minister and leader of the party. It is not surprising that the Queen therefore asked Lord Home to form a government in accordance with Macmillans' preference. Home must also have been a welcome choice to her, coming as he did from an ancient aristocratic Scots family of the social group with which she is most familiar.

By now it is clearly established that no one from the House of Lords can be Prime Minister – it is a matter of custom rather than a rule, for a member of the House of Lords would be unable to exercise the necessary control of the Commons, where real power lies. The Earl of Home therefore renounced his title and became plain Sir Alec Douglas-Home in order to be eligible for the Commons. Other hereditary peers have done the same, the best-known being the Labour MP Anthony Wedgwood Benn (Viscount Stansgate) and Quintin Hogg (Lord Hailsham). This situation reflects some of the fundamental social and political changes of the twentieth century: at the beginning of the century political power still lay largely with the landed aristocracy and wealthy industrialists, many of whom had received peerages. At the time of Elizabeth II's Silver Jubilee, to be a member of the House of Lords had become a distinct obstacle to political success. The Prime Minister who followed Sir Alec Douglas-Home, Labour Party leader Harold Wilson, soon put into effect his party's intention to end the creation of hereditary peerages except for

Queen Elizabeth during a visit to Silverwood Colliery, Yorkshire, 30 July 1975. The Queen, who was a shy retiring young woman at the beginning of her reign, has made a major contribution to the development of a modern, informal style of monarchy.

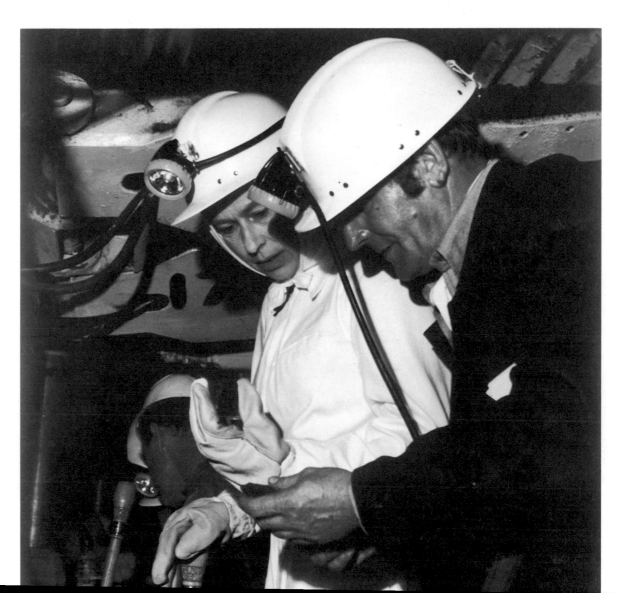

Above The Queen with the Yeoman Warders, usually known as the Beefeaters, at the Tower of London. The ceremonial axe and partisan lie crossed at the Queen's feet. Some of her antecedents' encounters with the Tower did not prove as entertaining as this one!

Left A dignified spectacle: the Queen on her way to the State Opening of Parliament.

Above The Queen, Queen Elizabeth the Queen Mother and the Prince of Wales assemble outside St George's Chapel, Windsor for the service of the Knights of the Garter.

Left Her Majesty and the Duke of Edinburgh participate in a time-honoured pageant: Trooping the Colour.

149

the Queen's immediate family. So much had the political climate changed since 1910 when the Liberals had threatened to swamp the House of Lords with newly created peers in order to ensure the passage of controversial social legislation that the Conservative Party was quite prepared to acquiesce to this measure.

The latter part of the Queen's reign has therefore seen the Upper Chamber evolve into something of a political 'siding' full of life peers, not a few of whom have been created in order to remove them from the active arena of the House of Commons without too much damage to their self-esteem. Although theoretically this subtly undermines the position of the sovereign, which is the most elevated hereditary position in the country, there seems to be no sign that the decreasing prestige of the House of Lords has affected attitudes to the Crown. Most other honours are also in the hands of the government of the day, as a convenient way of rewarding loyalty and service. Ironically it was Harold Wilson, whose high-minded principles brought about the end of hereditary peerages, who caused most controversy over his choice of recipients for major honours. The greatest criticism of all was for the people named in his resignation honours – several of whom were business men whose methods had been publicly criticized.

So although her powers are severely limited, Elizabeth II has had a real and important job to do: as travelling ambassador promoting Britain, as Head of the Commonwealth providing an acceptable focal point for such a loose-knit organization, as adviser to her government – a role which becomes more valuable as she extends her experience. While Britain remains a monarchy, and there is no reason to suspect it will not, the monarch has a positive, if rather indefinable, function. The same cannot be said so easily of the members of the monarch's family. They are confined by their status and yet required by public opinion to be seen to be earning their keep. It is no longer easy to live the life of 'the idle rich' without arousing criticism, and the media which have contributed to the monarch's prestige can work against those members of the monarch's family who are considered wanting.

The Queen's husband, the Duke of Edinburgh, has suffered from these disadvantages, with the additional difficulty of having been trained both at school and as a naval officer, to expect an active and worthwhile life. It has undoubtedly been hard on him to live his life in the shadow of his wife, and indeed when, at the end of 1956, he went on a four-month tour to Australia, which meant that he was absent for their wedding anniversary and for Christmas, the newspapers were full of hints of a possible marriage break-up. In February 1957 they met in Lisbon to begin the state visit to Portugal, and the rumours eventually fizzled out. Even so, the four-month tour undertaken by the Duke (which included a visit to the Arctic) showed very clearly his desire to put his energies to good use. Like Queen Victoria's husband, Prince Albert, so many years before, the Duke of Edinburgh has been deliberately denied any official role to play. His counterpart, Prince Bernhard of the Netherlands, husband of Queen Juliana, is not so rigorously denied a part to play in the running of the country. He is the head of the armed forces of the Netherlands.

HM Queen Elizabeth II and the Duke of Edinburgh, an official photograph taken for the occasion of the royal silver wedding anniversary.

Above Viscount Linley and Lady Sarah Armstrong-Jones at St George's Chapel with their parents.

Below Princess Margaret in her capacity as an official representative of the Crown.

Although the Queen has all the power and privileges of a male monarch, her husband does not automatically share her rank as a king's wife does. The Duke of Edinburgh was not crowned at the coronation as a king's wife is crowned queen. It was not until 1956 that he was created a prince of the United Kingdom and allowed to use the style and title of Royal Highness. Even then it was a personal honour conferred by the Queen and implied no political privileges or role. In spite of the drawbacks of his position, Prince Philip has managed to create for himself a definite place in what he once called 'the family firm'. Precisely because he has no official position, he can voice opinions which the Queen cannot, and he has often been a critic particularly of Britain's industrial performance. His speeches do not shun controversial topics, and it is assumed that he sometimes speaks for his wife as well as himself, thus allowing opinions to be made clear without compromising the Queen. In 1969 for example, as inflation began to bite and the industrial depression of the 1970s set in, he stated on American television that the Royal Family was 'going into the red' and remarked half-seriously, 'If nothing happens we shall have to – I don't know, we may have to move into smaller premises, who knows?'

His readiness to step down from traditional royal impartiality and his ready wit and gift for repartee have made him something of a favourite with the Press. This ability to get on with all types of people has made him an invaluable companion to the Queen on her many tours. It is unusual for her not to be accompanied by her husband when she goes abroad. The Prince also travels by himself, working hard as a publicist for Britain and seeking to encourage our commercial links with other countries. He has also found scope for his organizing skill and energy in his work for young people. He founded the Playing Fields Association and the Duke of Edinburgh Award Scheme, which encourages young people to help others and to develop a spirit of adventure and service. Another area in which he has been an active patron is the conservation of wild life. Indeed, Prince Philip has made the role of the monarchy as patron a much more vigorous function than it would otherwise have been and in his youth work in particular has continued the work of George VI.

The Queen's sister, Princess Margaret, has also suffered from the lack of any definite position while at the same time having been brought up to live a life set apart from the mainstream of ordinary people. She, like most other members of the present royal family, has taken a full share of the annual royal round of tree-planting, foundation-stone-laying, official openings, charity dinners and dances. In this she has performed a valuable service in widening the scope of occasions to which the monarchy lends its invaluable prestige and so extending the work of Elizabeth II beyond the number of functions at which she can actually be present. Nonetheless, although the life is superficially glamorous to the outsider, it is often repetitive and monotonous. Elizabeth II is fortunate in seeming to prefer a well-ordered existence with its annual repetition of events such as Trooping the Colour, State Opening of Parliament, Royal

Ascot and so on. Princess Margaret is clearly less well suited temperamentally to such a repetitive existence, and to lead it playing only a secondary role is undoubtedly more difficult.

Princess Margaret at a jamboree on the island of Mustique in the Windward Islands, West Indies.

In 1955 she felt the full weight of the disadvantages of being a royal princess when, bowing to public and private pressures, she renounced her intention to marry the divorcé Peter Townsend. Not only did she have to make her decision in a glare of publicity but it was a decision that was a problem only because of who and what she was. Her sister Elizabeth II is Head of the Church of England, which believes in marriage for life and does not allow divorced people to remarry in church. Had Princess Margaret married a divorced man, the situation would have been extremely embarrassing for the Queen. In addition there would have been the more practical disadvantage that public opinion may well have forced her to renounce both the privileges and financial advantages of her position. So in October 1955, to the relief of her immediate family, she made a public statement that she would not marry Townsend: 'Mindful of the Church's teaching that Christian marriage is indissoluble, and conscious of my duty to the Commonwealth, I have resolved to put these considerations before all others.' The rapid secularization of British society and the declining prestige of the Church in the quarter of a century which has elapsed since that decision was made, make it in some ways incomprehensible today.

A large family group taken in 1972 for the silver wedding.

However, what mattered then, and what still matters today, is not so much the opinion of the Archbishop of Canterbury, as the fact that the strength of the monarchy is now greatly dependent on its image as a family institution. Being the epitome of a secure and happy family contributes to its prestige and popularity. This was the unpalatable truth with which Edward VIII had to come to terms when he was seeking ways to reconcile his marriage to Mrs Simpson with remaining king. It was George VI's family as well as the King himself who were responsible fo re-establishing people's faith in the monarchy after the abdication crisis. So when Princess Margaret's marriage to Antony Armstrong-Jones, Earl of Snowdon, came to an end in 1978, she suffered again from publicity and criticism, even though for the majority of people the 1970s was an easy-going and permissive era which accepted situations far more unconventional than divorce with equanimity.

Almost inevitably therefore Princess Margaret's behaviour was used as an excuse for renewed criticism of royal finances and in

particular the Civil List. Nor is it surprising that such criticism has increased greatly in the more recent years of the Queen's reign when Britain has been suffering from inflation and the effects of a world recession in trade. One reason is that, because of this rapid inflation, the Civil List, which used to be decided at the beginning of the reign of a new monarch, now has to be reassessed every year and a new figure approved by Parliament. When Elizabeth II came to the throne, the Civil List was fixed at £475,000 annually. In 1970–1 an all-party House of Commons committee was set up to review this figure, which was by then inadequate, and to devise a new procedure for making sure that royal finance kept pace with the cost of living. Its proposal that the Civil List should be increased to £980,000 was agreed and implemented by the 1972 Civil List Act. A recommendation that royal finances should come under direct parliamentary control and a new body, the 'Commissioners of the Crown', set up to deal with them was rejected by only one vote.

In February 1975 yet another increase was agreed by Parliament, and the Civil List was raised to £1,400,000. Of this the Queen agreed to provide £150,000 from her personal fortune, and, as a concession to the prevailing economic climate, she also postponed alterations to Sandringham which were to have cost £200,000. By this time the need for an annual review and increase of the Civil List had become inescapable. It was perhaps fortunate that in 1975 Harold Wilson was Prime Minister: he was sympathetic to the financial difficulties of the Crown and also aware of the damaging effects on the Crown's reputation and loss of time in the Commons which would be caused by having to pass a new Civil List Act every year. The 1975 Civil List Act therefore did away with the need for a legislative decision by parliament every time an increase is required. Instead the increased sum is now included in the annual public expenditure estimates. In return the Queen now meets the payments of the Duke of Gloucester, the Duke of Kent, Princess Alexandra and Princess Alice, Countess of Athlone. This method has greatly simplified the whole procedure, and in 1978 the Civil List was increased to over two and a half million pounds distributed as follows:

	£
The Queen	1,950,000
	(estimated)
The Queen Mother	175,000
The Duke of Edinburgh	93,500
Princess Margaret	59,000
Princess Anne	60,000
Prince Andrew	17,282
Princess Alice (Gloucester)	30,000
Duke of Gloucester	39,000
Duke of Kent	60,000
Princess Alexandra	60,000
Princess Alice (Athlone)	6,500
	—————
	£2,550,262
	—————

The question of Crown finances always causes controversy, even though the government's annual expenditure on the Civil List is sometimes less than its subsidy to Covent Garden Opera House. However, the 1971 Commons select committee made it clear that the Civil List is not, as is so often assumed, a salary payable to the Queen and her family in return for which they are required to put in a set number of hours. (It was this misconception which caused so much of the acrimony towards Princess Margaret when a period of personal unhappiness and illness in 1977 and 1978 resulted in a reduction in the number of public engagements she fulfilled.) The committee made it clear that the Civil List is intended to reimburse those who receive money from it for the expenses they incur in the course of their official duties. A large part of it therefore goes simply to pay for the staff needed to enable the Royal Family to perform the tasks expected of it.

The Queen and Prince Philip kneel for the royal thanksgiving service. In front of Prince Philip lies the sword of state.

In fact approximately seventy-five per cent of the Queen's expenses for state visits abroad and the upkeep of the official residences, for example, are paid indirectly, by government departments. This rarely arouses criticism, precisely because it cannot be so easily presented by critics of the monarchy as an apparently grossly inflated salary. Indeed commonsense indicates that any Head of State would incur a similar cost. Another wrongful assumption is that the Queen's private expenses are paid for by the State. This again is untrue. Private expenditure by the Queen is met out of the Crown's private fortune. This fortune attracts its own criticism because it has achieved rapid growth largely by being immune from income tax.

The domed interior of St Paul's Cathedral, brimming with its distinguished congregation for the Jubilee thanksgiving service: the Children and Gentlemen of the Chapels Royal, the Vicars Choral, the Sergeant of the Vestry, the Most Excellent Order of the British Empire, the Most Distinguished Order of St Michael and St George, the Bath, the Garter, the Thistle and, of course, the Royal Family.

Left The Queen celebrated her Silver Jubilee by giving her people an extra day's holiday. Her day of celebration was not blessed with the glorious sunshine that had heralded Queen Victoria's Diamond Jubilee in 1897 but the pouring rain did not deter the crowds. Over 100,000 people clamoured outside Buckingham Palace to witness the Jubilee celebrations.

Opposite above The grey and puddled streets did not prevent the British people from holding street parties in vast and unexpected numbers.

Below left Princess Margaret and Earl Mountbatten of Burma return from the service of thanksgiving at St Paul's.

Opposite below The Jubilee thanksgiving service and walkabout was followed by a progress upriver from Greenwich. The Queen receiving a bouquet from a woman at Deptford who had witnessed Queen Victoria's Diamond Jubilee in 1897.

Nonetheless it does remove a large part of the burden of supporting the monarch from the government. One further point to be borne in mind when considering the controversial question of Crown finances is that ever since the reign of George III, when the Civil List was instituted, the sovereign has had to surrender the revenues of the Crown Estates in return for it.

The Silver Jubilee in 1977 was a demonstration that criticism of the Civil List is by no means the tip of a republican iceberg. In spite of continuing economic difficulties (for example, nearly 1,500,000 unemployed) which caused the Queen to ask for celebrations to be made without undue expenditure, there was an undoubted mood of festivity and enthusiasm throughout the country. Jubilee street parties were arranged; paving stones were painted red, white and blue; many houses hung out flags or displayed photographs of the Queen and Prince Philip, and souvenir-sellers made a fortune. Millions of foreign visitors came to London to be present for Jubilee Week. Over and over again people remarked privately as well as in the media on the way in which such royal events bolstered up a flagging sense of national pride and helped to inject a little life into a country which had developed a noticeable habit of dejected self-criticism. (A similar spirit on a smaller scale was apparent at the wedding of Princess Anne in 1973.)

It is this indefinable quality of monarchy that Elizabeth II has managed to retain throughout a reign which has already lasted longer than any of her predecessors' in this century. Over-exposure by the media might well have eroded the prestige of the monarchy, and pressure from an increasingly egalitarian society might have persuaded her to make too many concessions to 'ordinariness'. As it is, she has so far managed to achieve a fine balance: she has maintained the 'mystique' of monarchy by jealously guarding her privacy, yet she has made herself more accessible to her people than ever before. She has always disliked security measures which come between her and the people who have gathered to see her, and the so-called 'walkabouts' among the crowds which she first began on an early Australian tour have proved one of the greatest personal successes of her reign. Although in many ways Elizabeth II has seen the authority of the Crown whittled away, she has also helped it to evolve a different role, one which has been steadily growing in importance throughout the century.

This new role is as a symbol of unity, not simply, as it has always been, something to look up to but a symbol with which people can identify. In Elizabeth II and her family, people all over the world see the everyday events of their own lives – births, deaths, weddings, success and even occasionally failure – mirrored in an idealized and reassuring fashion. At the beginning of the century Edward VII once introduced his son, the future George V, as 'the last King of England'. Although Elizabeth II has revealed how crucial the actual personality of the individual monarch is, it is inconceivable three-quarters of a century later, that she would need to introduce her eldest son in the same way.

Opposite The Royal Family at Buckingham Palace.

CHAPTER SIX

The Queen's Children

Since the personality and personal qualities of the sovereign now count more than ever before in the continuing success of the monarchy, the Queen's children have a vital role to play in the future. Clearly the main task falls on the shoulders of the heir apparent, the Prince of Wales. Nevertheless his sister, Princess Anne, and his younger brothers Andrew and Edward, will also have to take their share. There are more occasions when a royal presence is required than Prince Charles himself could possibly attend, and the media can never have enough of royal 'stories' however trivial.

Prince Charles has had one advantage in his preparation for his eventual role which was denied his mother: he was educated at school from the age of eight. He attended first Hill House School in London and then followed in his father's footsteps to Cheam preparatory school and, at the age of thirteen, to Gordonstoun. Although these schools cater for boys of a similar background, and his education can scarcely be classified as 'roughing it', it has meant that Prince Charles was able to overcome at an early age the shyness which was such a disadvantage to his mother as a young woman. In many ways Prince Charles was unhappy at school, being neither an outstanding scholar nor, and this was a particular disadvantage at Gordonstoun, a natural leader. However he proved to be a late developer, and the turning-point in his school career was the two terms he spent as an exchange pupil at Timbertop, a branch of the famous Australian public school Geelong. 'I absolutely adored it,' he said later. 'I couldn't have enjoyed it more. The most wonderful experience I've ever had, I think. In Australia there is no such thing as aristocracy or anything like that.' In another interview, nearly ten years later, he said: 'More than any other experience those months opened my eyes. You are judged there on how people see you and feel about you.' Timbertop must take a lot of the credit for his undoubted ability nowadays to get on with all types of people.

On his return to Gordonstoun the Prince took and passed A level History and English and became 'Guardian', as the head-boy is known there. In October 1967 he went up to Cambridge as an undergraduate at Trinity College (where R. A. Butler was Master) to read archaeology with social anthropology. Unlike George VI, he stayed to take a degree and had the additional advantage of living in college, not a private house. Just as his schools were rarified, so the

Opposite Prince Charles, the heir apparent.

company he kept at college was rather limited. According to people who were up at the same time, his social circle was confined mainly to ex-public-school boys with upper-middle-class or aristocratic backgrounds. This may have been in some ways a missed opportunity to mix a little more with a wider range of people, but on the other hand it is quite understandable that the Prince should feel more at ease in the type of society to which he was accustomed. Certainly he put a lot of energy into his time at Cambridge. It was at this time that he began to emerge in the Press as a personality in his own right. A lot of coverage was given to his exploits with the college drama group, the Dryden Society, where, in two annual productions, he showed that he shares Princess Margaret's talent for amateur theatricals. Photographs of him clowning around in a dustbin rather endeared him to the public, as did reports of his sense of humour, based largely on a passion for a radio programme called 'the Goon Show'.

In 1969 his studies at Cambridge were interrupted by a term at the University of Wales at Aberystwyth, in preparation for his investiture on 1 July of that year as Prince of Wales. It was a tribute to his education as well as to his own rapidly maturing personality that he was able to cope so ably with the experience. There had been a growing movement for Home Rule in Wales, and the Queen and her advisers knew that the investiture was a calculated risk that might create more opposition than pro-monarchical fervour, so in a sense Prince Charles was being thrown to the lions when he was sent to Aberystwyth, as universities are naturally full of young idealists and the college was not short of supporters of Welsh Home Rule. As a precaution against possible reaction, a hundred Special Branch officers were stationed there. However the term was fairly uneventful, and Prince Charles impressed many people by his sincere intention to be a Prince of Wales in more than just name and by the amount of the notoriously difficult Welsh language he mastered while he was there. He showed too that he was aware of the situation and not cut off from reality. In an interview on 1 March 1969, St David's Day, Charles said, in what was his first radio interview:

It would be unnatural if one didn't feel any apprehension about it. But I think if one takes it as it comes, it'll be much easier. I expect at Aberystwyth there may be one or two demonstrations and as long as I don't get covered in too much egg and tomato I'll be alright. I've hardly been to Wales, and you can't expect people to be over-zealous about the fact of having a so-called English Prince to come amongst them and be frightfully excited.

The investiture itself was a great success. The last time such a ceremony had been held was for his great-uncle, the future Edward VIII, but the 1969 ceremony bore little resemblance to that occasion. There is in fact no official ceremonial for the investiture of the Prince of Wales. The rather quaint ceremonial devised for Prince Charles's investiture was really part of an elaborate public relations exercise, a chance to exploit once again the magic quality of royal ceremonial which is invariably followed by a spell of loyalist fervour among the majority of the population.

Prince Charles as a singing dustman. Charles acted in several revues during his three years at university where he showed that he was not afraid of playing the fool and having fun made of him.

The ceremony at Caernarvon Castle, which had been decorated by Lord Snowdon, the Constable of the Castle, was staged primarily with an eye to the television cameras. It was a simple yet impressive spectacle, particularly the moment when Prince Charles made his oath of allegiance to his mother as his feudal overlord. This is the one part of the ceremony that is of real antiquity, and the formula for the oath is the same as that used by Prince Edward to King George V at his coronation: 'I, Charles, Prince of Wales, do become your liege man of life and limb, and of earthly worship and faith and truth I will bear unto you, to live and die, against all manner of folks. So help me, God.' The investiture was followed by a tour of Wales and at the end of the entire venture Charles could feel that he had performed his first major engagement as part of the royal team well.

In the ten years which have followed he has improved still further on his natural aptitude for the task of royal representative. His manner has developed into something remarkably similar to that of his father, with the same apparent easiness of manner and ability to indulge in banter and repartee which is so appealing to the Press and public. Not surprisingly, since he is now considerably older than his mother was when she became Queen, his visits have become increasingly important, and much stress is laid on the fostering of

Above After being invested as Prince of Wales by his mother Charles made his oath of allegiance: 'I, Charles, Prince of Wales, do become your liege man of life and limb, and of earthly worship. . . .'

Above left The investiture of the Prince of Wales at Caernarvon Castle, 1 July 1969.

Above Charles kitted out for flight. His five-year spell in the services included an advanced flying course, from which he passed out above average.

Above right Charles's first command, of the minesweeper HMS *Bronington*, 1976. He proved an able and conscientious naval officer, and had a great capacity for practical jokes.

good trade relations with the countries he visits. This was an important part of his South American tour in March 1978.

On this tour, and on the tours to the United States and Australia which preceded it, much attention was given to the number of pretty girls who kissed him or were kissed by him. Inevitably as he grows older and passes the age of thirty, which he once declared was the optimum age to marry, the topic of whom he will eventually choose becomes a serious preoccupation. As he himself pointed out, the question is not just one of private preference when the person he marries will become the next queen. That person will have a lot of influence on the future popularity or otherwise of the monarchy, both at home and in the Commonwealth.

Prince Charles has escorted a number of well-chronicled girl friends, from the time when he met his first real girl friend at Cambridge, Lucia Santa Cruz, the daughter of a former Chilean Ambassador to London. Two were thought to be real contenders for the title of Princess of Wales: Lady Jane Wellesley, the daughter of the Duke of Wellington, and Princess Marie-Astrid of Luxembourg, probably because each of them comes from a background which would enable her to cope with the exigencies of the position of being the future queen. However, at the moment Prince Charles shows no obvious signs of 'settling down', and although he works fairly hard, he enjoys a pleasant life-style by any standard. He plays a lot of polo, hunts, shoots, goes to parties, skis and travels. All this is done from the base of his impressive country home, Chevening, a country estate of 3,500 acres in Kent, which was left to the nation by Lord Stanhope, with the express wish that it might become the official residence of the Prince of Wales.

The Prince is a wealthy man. He receives nothing from the Civil List as he has an income of nearly £250,000 a year from his estates as Duke of Cornwall. Although this is not taxed, he returns about half of it direct to the Exchequer.

However enjoyable his way of life is now, there is no doubt that in the future, as he becomes a middle-aged man, it is unlikely to prove totally satisfying, unless he can develop for himself a worthwhile job to do until the distant time when he is king. In 1971, after Cambridge, he predictably followed family tradition with several years in the services, first doing an advanced flying course with the RAF at Cranwell and then joining the Navy. Altogether he spent five years with the Navy, despite a tendency to sea-sickness, and was a conscientious officer. He took a course as a helicopter pilot, which he passed, and learned to parachute during a commando course with the Royal Marines. His training was frequently interrupted by official duties, and his achievements were therefore all the more commendable. In February 1976 he was given command of the minesweeper HMS *Bronington*, but in 1977 he resigned from the Navy to head the Silver Jubilee Appeal which raised money for young people's activities. Now that it is over, it remains to be seen if he will manage to fill his time in a constructive fashion without allowing his life to

Above Prince Charles at Royal Ascot with Davina Sheffield, a girl with whom he was associated for a couple of years. Marriage rumours abounded, but nothing came of it.

Left Charles seen here enjoying the company of Margaret Trudeau, wife of the Canadian Prime Minister, during the Prince's tour of Canada.

Left The Prince of Wales has had a succession of girl friends. In 1973 his attention was occupied with Lady Jane Wellesley, daughter of the Duke of Wellington. She is seen here with Charles at the Royal Polo Grounds, Windsor.

Below Prince Charles is an efficient and popular royal representative overseas. He is seen here at an Indian gathering at Blackfoot Crossing, Calgary, during his tour of Canada in 1977.

Opposite above Polo is Charles's favourite team game and he is an expert player on the field.

Opposite far left Cross-country ski-ing at Storlein, Sweden near the Norwegian border in 1969.

Opposite left The Prince of Wales as bowman: archery is one of Charles's many athletic accomplishments.

Prince Charles and Prince Andrew at the Scottish highland games held at Braemar near Balmoral, Aberdeenshire, Scotland.

Opposite Prince Andrew, a portrait taken on his coming-of-age at eighteen on 20 February 1978.

fritter away in a number of trivial occupations as his great-great-grandfather Edward VII did during his own long wait for the throne.

From time to time it has been suggested that the Queen might abdicate in favour of Prince Charles. Prince Philip has denied this. 'It has its attractions,' he has said, 'though it's not been thought of very seriously. The idea that Prince Charles would only be capable of making a contribution if he were sovereign is not really true.' Prince Charles is a highly personable, well-educated young man with an undoubted sense of duty and a flair for getting on with people. It remains to be seen whether his father is right and how he will use those talents in the apprenticeship he must serve before he is king.

The problem of finding satisfactory adult employment is of course even greater for Charles's younger brothers, Andrew, who was born in 1960, and Edward, born in 1964. At the moment it is a theoretical problem, for both are still being educated. Eventually, however, they will have to find something to do and in spite of their tremendous advantages will suffer the disadvantage of having to do what is expected of them by other people. The Duke of Gloucester, who, until the death of his elder brother, had been a promising architect, was forced to neglect his chosen career because of the demands on his time of being a royal duke rather than a relatively obscure younger brother. If this is the case for someone far down the line in the order of succession to the throne, it is unlikely that Andrew and Edward will be able to please themselves in how they spend their lives.

The traditional occupation for the younger sons of the sovereign has always been the armed forces, and this may well suit Prince Andrew. Unlike his elder brother he does not seem to have had any difficulties in coming to terms with the outside world and has fitted in well at his schools. Naturally good at physical activities, and what his father calls 'a natural boss', he has enjoyed the Gordonstoun life-style much more than Prince Charles did. He is a keen glider pilot and in 1978 joined Prince Charles on a parachute course. In 1977 he enjoyed an experience equivalent to Prince Charles's term at Timbertop when he spent six months in another Commonwealth country, Canada, at Lakefield College in the Kawartha Lake District about seventy miles east of Toronto. This choice, as with all the other schools chosen for the royal children, shows the influence of Prince Philip. The emphasis is always on reliance and physical prowess, and Lakefield is, if anything, even tougher than Gordonstoun or Timbertop. Of the Canadian school Prince Andrew said: 'The school is quite excellent and so are the facilities. But it's not just that – the boys here are quite terrific. They are different from chaps in England because they have a different outlook from a different country.' Prince Andrew got on well with the other boys at the school, for he has an attractive sense of humour which has made him a rival to his brother Charles for the title 'clown prince'. All these qualities, leadership, an ability to get on with people, physical prowess, indicate that he would be happy in the services. On the other hand, as Britain's importance as a world power decreases, so too does the prestige of her armed forces. A royal prince may once have been well occupied as an officer in the greatest

Above Prince Edward and his cousin Lady
Sarah Armstrong-Jones with the Queen at
Badminton Horse Trials.

Opposite above Prince Andrew in earnest
discussion with father Prince Philip during
horse trials.

Opposite below The younger royal children
with Princess Margaret and Queen Elizabeth
the Queen Mother at Clarence House on her
seventieth birthday. The children traditionally
lunch with their grandmother on her birthday.

navy in the world; being an officer in a navy which is rapidly declining
in numbers and influence is not quite the same thing. In 1978 it was
announced that Prince Charles is to spend some time familiarizing
himself with the workings of the city and of industry. It would be
interesting if Prince Andrew turned his attention in the same direction
and, instead of taking the obvious course, brought a little of the
invaluable royal prestige where it is most needed: to Britain's
economic performance.

Prince Edward's choice of career is not yet a matter for discussion.
He, like Prince Andrew, has been even more sheltered from publicity
than Prince Charles and Princess Anne were as children. Whatever he
chooses to do in the future, he will become more involved with
public duties and, as for all the family, they will inevitably form an
unavoidable part of his life although he is only third in line to the
throne. He and Prince Andrew are being gradually introduced to this
public life. They were at Montreal when Queen Elizabeth opened the
Olympic Games in 1976. They joined their parents for parts of the
Jubilee tour of the United Kingdom in 1977, including the potentially
fraught visit to Northern Ireland. In 1978 they returned again to
Canada for the opening of the Commonwealth Games. Prince
Edward, like Prince Andrew, shows every sign of growing into an
extremely attractive young man, and both of them will undoubtedly
be an asset to the monarchy in the future.

Princess Anne competing in a cross-country event. The Princess is a dedicated horsewoman of Olympic class.

As her younger brothers grow up and take their share of royal duties, Princess Anne may well choose to cut down on her own public appearances. She has had an unpredictable relationship with both Press and public. In 1969, after taking two A levels at Benenden School, where she had been a pupil for six years, she began to make public appearances. Her first solo public engagement was at the annual presentation of shamrock to the Irish Guards. She coped fairly well with the undoubted strain of being a public person but showed little understanding of the importance of keeping the Press happy. The twentieth-century monarchy stays where it is because people like it, and making sure they continue to like it requires hard work from all the members of the Royal Family. As objects of admiration they cannot afford to antagonize their public or the Press which brings them to their public. It took Princess Anne rather longer than the other members of her family to realize that her privileges require the price of playing the game and of behaving irreproachably at all times. Nearly a decade after some initial incidents when she was often seen scowling and unfriendly and when she was prone to answer questions in an offhand manner, the Princess seems to have come to terms with

what is expected of her. Photographs now inevitably show her smiling, and although she cannot resist answering back when heckled by anti-blood sport demonstrators, she behaves impeccably on all other occasions. Being the only girl, she is a useful asset to the Royal Family, as the enthusiasm and sentiment displayed at the time of her wedding in 1973 showed.

She has also earned genuine respect and admiration for her riding ability. In 1971 she won the European Individual Three-Day Event Championship with Doublet, a horse bred by the Queen, and was chosen as Sports Personality of the Year. She failed to qualify for the 1972 Olympics but was in the British Team at the 1976 Olympics at Montreal. Her husband, Mark Phillips, is also a world-class rider. Shortly after the birth of their son Peter, Princess Anne was back in the saddle, and she competed at the Badminton Horse Trials five months later. She was also quick to begin taking on her share of public engagements again.

In 1976 the Queen bought Princess Anne and her husband a large house and estate in the Cotswolds called Gatcombe Park. A little later the adjoining farm was added. Mark Phillips, who did not take a title

Above Gatcombe Park, Gloucestershire, the home the Queen bought for Princess Anne and Mark Phillips.

Left Queen Elizabeth and Princess Anne with baby Peter Mark Phillips, born 15 November 1977. This was one of the first official pictures of the new royal baby.

Opposite Princess Anne and Captain Mark Phillips at Buckingham Palace after their wedding in November 1973.

when he married the Queen's daughter, left the army in 1978 as it became clear that accompanying his wife on public engagements would prevent his getting enough active soldiering to make a proper career in the army. He will farm the Cotswold estate, and the couple have plans to breed horses there. Princess Anne has therefore managed to achieve a life-style which suits her ideally. Her own contentment makes her more attractive to the public, who enjoy seeing photographs of her as a happy mother with her baby. Paradoxically therefore it may be that, as she achieves what she wants, she becomes more the person that the public wants and, rather

Above Balmoral Castle, set amidst the glorious landscape of Aberdeenshire, Scotland, is the country retreat of the Royal Family, a favourite place for relaxing and getting away from the pressures of public life.

Above right Prince Philip and Princess Anne relaxing at Balmoral, 1972.

Right Prince Edward with a friend at Balmoral Castle in 1972.

than allowing her country life in Gloucestershire to make her more reclusive, she will be happy to stay on in public life.

The story of Britain's monarchy in the twentieth century must be counted a success simply because it still exists, and shows no signs of coming to an end in the forseeable future. The ritual, pomp and ceremony which are associated with royalty clearly appeal to something very fundamental in human nature which is not satisfied by the more rational alternative of an elected Head of State. The living representative of a family like the British Royal Family, which can trace its ancestry back to the time before the Conquest, and which is therefore intimately associated with the country's history for over a thousand years, forms a natural focus for the loyalty and allegiance of the people. Despite this there have been times during the present century when it seemed that the monarchy might well come to an end. Instead it is more secure than ever – not because it is politically stronger than ever before but precisely because it is not. The success of Britain's monarchs has been due to their flexibility and ability to accept gracefully their changing role, while those European dynasties which fought tooth and nail for every last vestige of absolute power are now gone and almost totally forgotten.

At the same time the British Royal Family has not been tempted towards the opposite extreme – the Queen is not to be glimpsed popping down to Harrods on her bicycle to do the family shopping. Indeed this would detract greatly from her prestige, despite the fact that we live in a much more equal society now than we did in 1901 when Edward VII came to the throne. So while it has been fortunate that George V was able to establish a working relationship with his Labour government or that George VI did not try to interfere in the independence of India, it is perhaps equally important that they did not compromise the dignity and mystique which remain an essential part of the Crown's strength today.

As it is the British monarchy is unique: it has survived the threats to its continued existence and emerged as an institution whereby Elizabeth II certainly does not have the dictatorial power of her ancestor Elizabeth I but is, in her own way, just as essential. For the paradox is that though the Crown has no real power, if it disappeared it would leave a very big gap to be filled in both our national life and our government. So well has the Royal Family evolved a new twentieth-century role for itself that if it did not exist we would have to invent it!

Prince Charles with his cousin Lady Sarah Armstrong-Jones at Balmoral, 1972.

Acknowledgments

Photographs and illustrations are supplied or are reproduced by kind permission of the following:

The pictures on pages 2–3, 9, 10, 11, 20, 23, 24–5, 35, 46–7, 50–1, 54, 60–1, 73, 97 above, 99, 126–7, 127 are reproduced by gracious permission of HM the Queen. The picture on page 52 is reproduced by gracious permission of HM Queen Elizabeth the Queen Mother.
Gilbert Adams: 86
Associated Press: 6 left, 86, 113 below, 118, 119, 177 below
Courtesy of Sir Cecil Beaton: 91, 138
British Library: 30, 36 left
British Tourist Authority: 101, 178
Camera Press: Endpapers, 141, 144, 148–9, 150–1, 154–5, 158 top left, 161, 165, 168 below right, 171, 175 above, 176, 177 above, 179 above, 181
Castle Museum and Art Gallery, Nottingham (Photo John Webb): 65
Conservative Party Library: 39 left and right
Cooper-Bridgeman Library: 59, 106–7
John Fleming: 12–13
Fox Photos: 121 below, 123, 139 top, 143, 172, 174
Guildhall Library: 56, 67
John Hall: 58 above
Illustrated London News: 15, 24 left, 75, 80
Imperial War Museum: 64, 66, 68, 70, 110–11, 110 below, 112 above, 113 above (Photo Eileen Tweedy), 115
Keystone Press: 93, 105, 114, 139 below left, 156, 158 below, 158 top right, 165
Leeds City Council: 77
London Express Pictures: 153
London Museum: 32–3, 40, 58
Mander and Mitchenson Collection: 26
Mansell Collection: 45, 98
Mary Evans Picture Library: 36 right, 37, 41
National Coal Board: 147
National Maritime Museum: 48–9
National Portrait Gallery: 4, 6 right, 17, 21, 38, 42, 72, 82 above and below
Popperfoto: 53, 63, 71, 78, 79, 81, 83 below, 88, 89, 92, 95, 102 above and below, 103, 104, 116–17, 121 above, 122, 129, 130–1, 132, 133, 135, 164
Press Association: 84, 85
Radio Times Hulton Picture Library: 28, 29, 31, 87, 90, 96, 97 below, 100
Rex Features: 142, 152 below
John Scott: 134, 137 above and below, 139 below right, 145, 149 above and below, 152, 166 left, 167 above and below, 168 above, 169 above, 170, 172 above, 173
Société Jersiaise: 27
The Sunday Times: 1, 159 below
Syndication International: 7, 124, 136 above and below, 140, 146, 148 below, 157, 159 above, 166 right, 168 below left, 169, 175 below, 179
Tate Gallery: 108–9, 112 below

Picture research by Shelley Harper and Annette Brown.

Index